A SHARED STRUGGLE

Stories of Palestinian & Irish Hunger Strikers

Norma Hashim | Yousef M. Aljamal

First published in 2021 by
An Fhuiseog
55 Falls Road
Belfast BT12 4PD
Ireland

A Shared Struggle

Supervised by
Norma Hashim
(All contributions with the permission of their owners and all pictures and illustrations courtesy of their owners)

Translated by
Yousef M. Aljamal

Revised and edited by
Asad Abu Sharkh & Danny Morrison

Design and layout by Low Seong Chai

ISBN978-1-8384835-0-0

Printed in India

Endorsements for
A Shared Struggle

"Colonialism and occupation are the denial of peoples'
right to self-determination and freedom. The Irish and
Palestinian people have had long experience of this. In
the struggle for liberty international solidarity between
oppressed and dispossessed peoples is hugely important. In
this joint Palestinian/Irish republican initiative we witness
the parallels between heroic struggles for freedom and the
commonality of resistance against seemingly overwhelming
military might particularly by those imprisoned in the cause
of freedom for their homeland."

~ **Gerry Adams**, Ex-political prisoner, former President Sinn Féin

"Because justice is indivisible, the Irish and Palestinian
quest for freedom followed the same trajectory of pain
and resistance and was met with the same, ever predictable
response of colonial oppression and state violence. The
prisoners, in both cases, serve as a microcosm of entire
collective experiences. Political prisoners are the victims
and the freedom fighters, the agitators, the intellectuals, and
the leaders of their communities. Their stories stand at the
heart of the shared narrative of both nations. This book is a
beautiful tribute to the heroic men and women of Palestine

and Ireland. It is an essential read for those wishing to understand why servitude is never an option, and why the struggle for freedom is worth all the painful sacrifices."

~ **Ramzy Baroud**, Author of *These Chains Will Be Broken: Palestinian Stories of Struggle and Defiance in Israeli Prisons*

"Hunger strikes are the last desperate weapon for political prisoners denied justice. For many years, there has been solidarity between the Palestinians, South Africans fighting apartheid and the struggle for Irish unity. That mutual support is active now and needed more than ever, as the oppression of the Palestinians becomes ever more brutal. This is an important book, and I'm sure it will be widely read."

~ **Ken Loach**, Award-winning film director

"One of the painful but inevitable repercussions of being colonised is the existence of political prisoners. Incarcerated for daring to fight for freedom and justice, the pain is multiplied when their suffering is completely ignored by the international community. The heroism of Palestinian and Irish political prisoners is no different from that of Nelson Mandela and other fighters against the apartheid regime of South Africa. But while the latter group is adulated and admired by all, Palestinian political prisoners are still considered terrorists by most Western governments, forcing them to resort to hunger strikes to obtain justice and freedom from the yoke of oppression. Norma Hashim and Yousef M. Aljamal's book is not only unique but also extremely valuable because it helps us to understand their suffering by describing the first-hand experiences of Irish and Palestinian hunger strikers."

~ **Prof Nazari Ismail**, Chairman of BDS Malaysia

"This is a significant book as the richness of the diverse prisoners and cases from Ireland and Palestine help the readers to understand their contribution to the national movement in both countries."

~ **Ibrahim Natil**, Academic and human rights activist

"*A Shared Struggle* is an important contribution to the literature of people from Palestine and Ireland telling their own stories, in their own words. We are reminded in these pages of the immense brutality being visited on the Palestinian people on a daily basis, both physically and psychologically, and how resistance to the occupation takes places in many forms. The Israeli apartheid state is, as some have argued, worse than apartheid South Africa and I hope this book will inspire more people to get involved in international solidarity and join the movement for Boycott, Divestment and Sanctions (BDS)."

~ **Richard Boyd Barrett**, People Before Profit TD

My refusal to take food was not a suicide attempt as it was portrayed by the Israeli occupation media, but rather it was a legitimate defence tool in which I used my body to impose my demands and highlight my case as a political prisoner who has been stripped off his dignity and freedom. Despite my prior knowledge of the risk of going on a hunger strike and that I might lose my life the same as some Irish hunger strikers did, I decided to go on with my hunger strike because every martyr who falls on this path is a light to those who seek freedom. I encourage you to read this book to learn more about the experiences of Palestinian and Irish hunger strikers. One line on the wall of my cell read "Read until your sight goes away so that your vision strengthens." This book is an important read."

~ **Mahmoud Al-Sarsak**, Palestinian footballer and
former hunger striker in Israeli jails

"This collection of first person accounts from Irish and Palestinian hunger strikers is compelling – a mix of powerful stories, poems, and photographs. Together these primary documents provide an essential political history that draws on a long tradition of protest with urgent moral force and challenges the criminalisation of those incarcerated for their fierce resistance to colonial violence. Shared struggles, indeed!"

~ **J. Kēhaulani Kauanui**, author of *Paradoxes of Hawaiian Sovereignty*

"With its harrowing accounts of the bravery and strength of Palestinian and Irish republican hunger strikers, this book will inspire people to support the freedom struggles of oppressed people all over the world and will shine a light on the brutal Israeli apartheid regime. When people are prepared to sacrifice their own lives for a cause they will never be defeated."

~ **Senator Frances Black**, Dublin, Ireland

Contents

A protester holding a cartoon of hunger striker Muhammad Al-Qeeq which condemns the deafening silence of the international community.

Foreword

Richard Falk

DESPERATE circumstances give rise to desperate behaviour. If by states, extreme violent behaviour tends to be rationalised as 'self-defence,' 'military necessity,' or 'counterterrorism,' and governmental claims of legal authorisation tend to be upheld by judicial institutions. If even nonviolent acts of resistance by individuals associated with dissident movements occur, then the established order and its supportive media will routinely describe such acts as 'terrorism,' 'criminality,' 'political extremism,' and 'fanaticism,' and the behaviour is criminalised, or at best exposed to scorn by sovereign states and their civil society establishment. Statist forms of combat almost always rely on violence to crush an enemy, while the desperation of resistance sometimes takes the form of inflicting hurt upon the self so as to shame an oppressor to relent or eventually even surrender, not due to empathy or a change of heart, but because fearful of alienating public opinion, intensifying resistance, losing international legitimacy, facing sanctions. It is against such an overall background that we should understand the role of the hunger strike in the wider context of resistance against all forms of oppressive, exploitative, and cruel governance. The long struggles in Ireland and Palestine are among the most poignant instances of such political encounters that gripped the moral imagination of many persons of conscience in the years since the middle of the prior century.

Those jailed activists who have recourse to a hunger strike, either singly or in collaboration, are keenly aware that they are choosing an option of last resort, which exhibits a willingness to sacrifice their body and even their life itself for goals deemed more important. These goals usually involve either safeguarding dignity and honour of a subjugated people or mobilising support for a collective struggle on behalf of freedom, rights, and equality. A hunger strike is an ultimate form of non-violence, comparable only to politically motivated acts of self-immolation, physically harmful only to the self, yet possessing in certain circumstances unlimited symbolic potential to change behaviour and give rise to massive displays of discontent by a population believed to be successfully suppressed. Such desperate tactics have been integral to the struggles for basic rights and resistance to oppressive conditions in both Palestine and Ireland.

An unacknowledged, yet vital, truth of recent history is that symbolic politics have often eventually controlled the outcomes of prolonged struggles against oppressive state actors that wield dominant control over combat zones and uncontested superiority in relation to weapons and military capabilities. And yet despite these hard power advantages thought decisive in such conflict, the struggle from below persists, often at great cost, yet in the end surprises the world, and sometimes itself, by prevailing. It may be helpful to remember that it was the self-immolation of Buddhist monks in Saigon during the 1960s that was considered 'a scream of the culture' in defiant reaction to the American led military intervention, which many credited with reversing the course of the conflict. It led Vietnamese scholars to interpret these extreme acts of solitary individuals, endowed with the highest civilisational credentials of moral authority, as shifting the balance of forces in Vietnam in ways that then and there doomed the seemingly irresistible American military resolve to control the political future of Vietnam. These acts of self-immolation didn't end the war, but to those with insight into Vietnamese culture it did signal an outcome contrary to what the war planners in Washington confidently expected. Tragically before Washington brought itself to acknowledge defeat, the Vietnam war persisted for a decade, ravaging the land and bringing great suffering to the people of Vietnam. Self-immolation, setting oneself on fire as an irreversible instance of self-sacrifice, carries the analogous logic of a hunger strike to a final conclusion. Depending on the actor and context, self-immolation can be interpreted either as an expression of hopeless despair or as a desperate appeal for a just peace.

It was the self-immolation of a simple fruit and vegetable vendor, Mohamed Bouazizi in the Tunisian town of Sidi Bouzid on 17 December, 2010 that called attention to the plight of the Tunisian people, igniting a nationwide uprising that drove a corrupt dictator, Ben Ali, from power.

Bouazizi, without political motivation or spiritual authority of the Buddhist monks, sparked populist mobilisations that swept across the Arab world in 2011. Somehow Bouazizi's entire personal self-immolation was the spark that set the region ablaze. Such a reaction could not have been predicted and was not planned, yet afterwards it was interpreted as somehow activating dormant revolutionary responses to intolerable underlying conditions.

Without doubt, the supreme example of triumphant symbolic politics in modern times was the extraordinary resistance and liberation movement led by Gandhi that merged his individual hunger strikes unto death with spectacular nonviolent forms of collective action (for instance, the Salt March of 1930), accomplishing what seemed impossible at the time, bringing the British Empire to its knees, and by so doing, restoring independent statehood and sovereignty to colonised India.

Both the oppressed and the oppressors learn from past successes and failures of symbolic politics. The oppressed view such behaviour as an ultimate and ennobling approach to resistance and liberation. Oppressors learn that wars are often not decided by who wins on the battlefield or jail house but by the side that gains a decisive advantage symbolically in what I have previously called 'legitimacy wars.' With this acquired knowledge of their vulnerability to such tactics, oppressors fight back, defame and use violence to destroy by any means the will of the oppressed, and their global support network, to resist, especially if the stakes involve giving up the high moral and legal ground. The Israeli leadership learned, especially, from the collapse of South African apartheid not to take symbolic politics lightly. Israel has been particularly unscrupulous in its responses to symbolic challenges to its abusive apartheid regime of control. Israel, with U.S. support, has mounted a worldwide defamatory push back against criticism at the UN or from human rights defenders around the world, shamelessly playing 'the anti-Semitic card' in its effort to destroy nonviolent solidarity efforts such as the pro-Palestinian BDS Campaign modelled on an initiative that had mobilised worldwide opposition to South African apartheid. Notably, in the South African case, the BDS tactic was questioned for effectiveness and appropriateness, but its organisers and most militant supporters were never defamed, much less criminalised. This recognition of the potency of symbolic politics by Israel has obstructed the Palestinian liberation struggles despite what would seem to be the advantageous realities of the post-colonial setting.

Israel's version of an apartheid regime evolved as a necessary side effect of establishing an exclusivist Jewish state in an overwhelmingly non-Jewish society. This Zionist project required that the Palestinian people experience the agonies of colonialist dispossession and displacement in their own homeland. Israel learned from South Africa techniques of racist hierarchy and repression, but they were also aware of the vulnerabilities of oppressors to sustained forms of non-violence that validated the persevering resistance of those oppressed. Israel is determined not to repeat the collapse of South African apartheid, which explains not only repression of resistors but sustained efforts to achieve the demoralisation of supporters that comprise the global solidarity movement, especially those in the West where Israel's geopolitical backup is situated.

A similar reality existed in Northern Ireland where the memories of colonies lost to weaker adversaries slowly taught the UK lessons of accommodation and compromise, which led the leaders in London to shift abruptly their focus from counterterrorism to diplomacy, with the dramatic climax of the Good Friday Agreement in 1998. Israel is not the UK, and the Irish are not the Palestinians. Israel shows no willingness to grant the Palestinian people their most basic rights, even withholding COVID-19 vaccines, yet even Israel does not want to be humiliated in ways that can arouse international public opinion to move from the rhetoric of censure toward the imposition of sanctions. The Israeli Prison Service doesn't want Palestinian hunger strikers to die in captivity, not because of their empathy, but to avoid bad publicity. To prevent such outcomes, Israeli prison authorities will often attempt forced feeding, but if that fails, as it usually does, then they will bend the rules, make some concessions, including even arrange a release when it is feared that a hunger striker is at the brink of death. Palestinian prospects are more dependent than ever on waging and winning victories in the domain of symbolic politics, and Israel, with the help of the United States, will go to any length to hide tactical defeats of this sort in this longest of legitimacy wars.

It is against such a background that these writings were collected, with Palestinian and Irish contributions interspersed throughout the volume to underscore the essential similarity of these two epic anti-colonial struggles. What gives *A Shared Struggle* its authority and persuasive power is the authenticity derived from words of those brave men and women who chose to undertake hunger strikes in situations of desperation and experienced not only their own spirit-enhancing ordeal but the pain of loss of nearby martyred fallen comrades, grieving families, and their common effort to engage the wider struggles for rights and freedom being carried on outside the prison walls. Despite the vast differences in their respective struggles against oppression, the similarities of response created the deepest of bonds, especially of the Irish toward the Palestinians whose oppressive reality was more severe, and has proved more enduring. The inspirational example of the Irish hunger strikers who did not abandon their quest for elemental justice at the doorstep of death was not lost on the Palestinians. At the end of their protest in 1981 the Irish prisoners obtained formal recognition of their political movement. They also were finally granted recognition by the British that Irish resisters deserved to be treated as 'political prisoners,' and not common criminals, after the Good Friday Agreement when they were released from prison, a political amnesty in all but name. The struggle for Irish independence has not let up, continuing in all of Ireland as an unresolved quest.

Ever since visiting Belfast two years ago I have been struck by how the Irish revolutionaries, despite these vast differences in circumstances and goals, regard their struggle as being reproduced in its essential character by the Palestinian struggle, and have a robust solidarity movement that regards Palestinian freedom as one of the incomplete aspects of their own struggle. The wall murals in the Catholic neighbourhoods of Belfast exhibited these affinities, recognising that oppression is not confined within the sovereign space of nations, but is a transnational reality with a boundaryless community of dedicated individuals. Solidarity and opposition express an unarticulated and largely unacknowledged global humanism. While the Palestinian challenge may be more epic in quality and intensity, the Irish struggle was also waged as a matter of life and death, and even more fundamentally, as an insistence that humiliation, indignity, and servitude were unendurable conditions that produced and justified martyrdom.

Among the great differences in these two national narratives that form the background of these separate renderings of the hunger strikes concerns the impacts of the international context, and especially the role of the United States. With regard to Ireland, American public and even elite opinion was strongly supportive of Catholic resistance in Northern Ireland, and the U.S. mediational role was exercised with an impressive spirit of neutrality. With respect to Israel, the U.S. pretends to play a similar role as intermediary or 'honest broker,' yet with zero credibility. It should surprise no objective observer that these diplomatic manoeuvres associated with a faux peace process produced only frustration and disappointment for the Palestinians, in part, due to Washington's unabashed and unconditional material and diplomatic partisanship, including siding with Israel even when it flagrantly violates international law or repudiates the UN consensus on the contours of a just peace. Such futile diplomacy allowed Israel to continue building its unlawful settlements for year after year, compromising Palestinian territorial prospects and resulting in not a single adverse consequence for Israel.

The media treatment of the two struggles reinforced this disparity. The Irish hunger strikes were given generally sympathetic prominence in mainstream media outlets, with Bobby Sands' name and martyrdom known and respected throughout the world. In contrast, outside of Palestinian circles only those most engaged activists in solidarity efforts are even aware that lengthy and life threatening Palestinian hunger strikes have repeatedly occurred in Israeli prisons during the last several decades.

This denial of international coverage to such nonviolent resistance acts helps reinforce Israeli oppression and uphold the Israeli anti-terrorist narrative, and should be viewed as a kind of transnational complicity. Naked power and geopolitical 'correctness,' rather than elemental morality is allowed to dominate the discourse. In the background is the bankruptcy of liberal Zionism. For many years, leading liberal journalists, such as Tom Friedman of the *New York Times*, were counselling the Palestinians that if they gave up violence, and appealed to Israeli conscience by having recourse to nonviolent forms of resistance, their political grievances would be addressed in a responsible manner. Palestinians responsively launched the first intifada in 1987, and soon realised that those meddlesome liberal establishment well-wishers in the West were quickly muted as soon as Israel responded violently, seeking to crush this most impressive nonviolent and spontaneous mobilisation of those Palestinians fed up with living under the rigours of prolonged occupation.

Silence about Palestinian hunger strikes reduces the global impact of these expressions of desperation, which makes this publication of additional significance. It exposes readers to a series of separate stories of heroism under intolerable conditions of Irish and Palestinian imprisonment. This collection also offers a corrective to the virtual media blackout in the West that denies coverage to Palestinian resistance including even, as with hunger strikes, when resistance turns away from violence, and expresses a desperate last resort. Again, the contrasting international media binge coverage of the Irish hunger strikes definitely contributed to the liberating Irish diplomatic breakthrough that might otherwise not have occurred, or at least not as soon as it did.

We notice in these stories collected here, that the Irish contributions situate their recourse to hunger strikes protesting prison conditions more explicitly in the wider struggle of the IRA, while Palestinians stories tell more graphically of the agonies of prolonged imprisonment in Israeli prisons. Our attention is drawn to the denial of minimal international standards of treatment, including failures of medical treatment, bad food quality, denial of family visits, inadequate exercise, and sadistic prison responses ranging from force-feeding to tempting hungry strikers by placing tantalising foods in prison cells. Yet both Irish and Palestinian styles of witnessing emanate from the same source – how to respond to the desperation felt by intolerable abuse in conditions of imprisonment, and yet carry on the wider struggle for freedom and rights that landed them in prison.

In reading these harrowing statements of broken families and broken hearts, we should not be deceived into thinking that we are reading only about events in the past. There are currently about 4,500 Palestinian prisoners, including 350 imprisoned under 'administrative detention' provisions copied from the British Mandate colonialist administration of Palestine, under which Palestinian activists and suspects can be jailed indefinitely without any specific charges or even a show of some evidence of wrongdoing. Many of the individual hunger strikes take this dire step of a hunger strike without an end date to protest against the acute and arbitrary injustices associated with administrative detention, which appears to be a technique used by Israel to demoralise the Palestine people to an extent that makes their resistance seem useless.

Maher Al-Akhras was close to death in an Israeli prison when freed on 26 November, 2020, having mounted a hunger strike for an incredible period of 103 days as a specific protest against being held under administrative detention, that is, without any charges of criminality. Hardly anyone outside of Palestine and the Israeli Prison Service knows about his ordeal. Al-Akhras' words when teetering on the brink of death encapsulate the common core of these unforgettable shared stories: "my hunger strike is in defence of Palestinian prisoners and of my people who are suffering from the occupation and my victory in the strike is a victory for the prisoners and my Palestinian people." In other words, although such an extreme act of self-sacrifice, while being intensely individual, is above all an expression of solidarity with others locked within the prison walls but at the same time often the only form of resistance available to an imprisoned political militant. Such a commitment has its concrete demands relating to prison conditions, but it should also be understood as a metaphor encouraging a greater commitment by all of us, wherever situated, to the struggle that needs to be sustained until victory by those on the outside who are daily subjugated to the policies and practices of the oppressor state.

These stories are here to be read, but the publication of such a collection is also a global solidarity initiative supportive of the Palestinian struggle. The suffering and rightlessness of the Palestinian people has gone on far too long. We now know that the UN and traditional diplomacy have failed to achieve a just solution. Given these circumstances, it becomes clear that only the people of the world possess the will and potentially the capabilities, to bring justice to Palestine. It is an opportunity and responsibility posing a challenge to all of us. We need to find what ways are available to support those brave and dedicated Palestinians who have paid for so long the price of resisting Israeli oppression.

Palestinian and Irish hunger strikers who contributed their stories to this memorable volume deserve the last word here. Mohammed Al-Qeeq says this, "It is not just about my freedom, but rather the freedom of every soul who curses the injustice as I do." From Mohamad Alian these words, "In our minds the prison became our cemetery." And from Pat Sheehan this assessment of the hunger strikes, "It was, and remains, one of the most defining and momentous periods in Irish history." Finally, Hassan Safadi, "The look on the faces of the Zionist officers who wanted me dead, will never leave me, but I stared right back at them."

Richard Falk
Yalikavak, Turkey
24 February, 2021

Richard Falk is Albert G. Milbank Professor Emeritus of International Law at Princeton University, currently Chair of Global Law, Queen Mary University of London, and Research Fellow, Orfalea Center of Global Studies, University of California, Santa Barbara. Falk served as UN Special Rapporteur on Human Rights in Occupied Palestine (2008-2014). He is the author of numerous books on international politics and governance. His political memoir, Public Intellectual: Life of a Citizen Pilgrim *was published by Clarity Press in February 2021.*

Introduction

Asad Abu Sharkh and Danny Morrison

Asad Abu Sharkh

LOCATED in two different continents, Palestine and Ireland suffered from the same brutal British colonialism. The brutality of the British colonisation was not only reflected in the way they savagely invaded, occupied and colonised the two countries but also in the racist laws they imposed on the Palestinian and Irish people.

The British colonisers did all they could to subjugate, humiliate and dehumanize both peoples to impose total surrender, resignation and submission. By creating a master-slave or oppressor–oppressed dichotomy, with the colonists as supreme masters, they intended to deepen the inferiority complex among the colonized people to make them always feel that they are a lesser race or a surplus people and unfit for self-government.

The main problems which Ireland and Palestine are still suffering from are mostly attributable to British colonization.

In Ireland, they drove a wedge between northern and southern Ireland and created divisive realities and new facts on the ground depicting the conflict as "the sectarian Catholic IRA killing the Protestant RUC" with Britain as an "honest broker," acting to keep apart "the two warring religious tribes."

In Palestine the British issued the infamous Balfour Declaration of 1917 by Foreign Secretary Arthur Balfour (known in Ireland as 'Bloody Balfour'). It shamelessly, disgracefully and unilaterally decided to hand over Palestine to a third party: the Zionist movement. The plan was to uproot and expel the Palestinian people, and to bring in Zionists – exclusively of Jewish ethnicity – from all over the world through a process of settlement-building in Palestine, similar to the plantation process the British had carried out in Ireland.

Under the British Mandate, the High Commissioner to Palestine, Herbert Samuel, who earlier as Home Secretary had overseen the internment of 2,000 Irish people allegedly involved in the Easter Rising and approved the hanging of Irish patriot Roger Casement, deliberately facilitated mass Zionist immigration to the country.

He carried out a ruthless iron-fist policy against any sort of resistance, which included ordering air strikes against Palestinians protesting against the Zionist colonial policies.

The Zionist authorities inherited their brutality from the British colonizers. One legal adviser to the Colonial Office, Gratten Bushe, warned that "repression by force is repeating the mistake which was made in Ireland." His advice was ignored. Military commanders were assured that they could take "whatever measures are necessary," which included demolishing much of Jaffa's old city, imposing collective punishment on villages and mass detention in labour camps. Needless to say it was Churchill who sent the Black and Tans to repress and persecute the Palestinian people as they did in Ireland.

Apartheid Israeli and British prisons, whether it is Nafha or Long Kesh, are more 'slaughter houses' than prisons, because the cages, the cells, are built in such a way as to cause maximum physical and psychological damage and traumas, and consequently slow death and ultimately physical death inside or outside the prison. (Since 1967 Israel has also had a practice of stealing and secretly burying the bodies of Palestinian activists in graves unmarked except by numbers – 'Numbers Graveyards' – and keeping the dead bodies of prisoners until their sentences expire.)

Many prisons have underground cells for solitary confinement. They are surrounded by high walls equipped with watch towers, CCTV, heavily armed soldiers and guard dogs. Some of these notorious prisons are built in the heart of the desert such as the Negev Prison where cells are unbearably hot in the summer and freezing cold in the winter. Prisoners are denied suitable bedding and covers, as well as basic human rights and needs.

Palestinian prisoners are held in more than twenty-two prisons and detention centres throughout occupied Palestine, which are heavily and extensively patrolled and guarded by the most sophisticated technological equipment that monitor the inmates around the clock.

Palestinian political prisoners have staged many hunger strikes: the 1969 hunger strike continued for eleven days in Beit-Lid and Ramla Prisons and resulted in the death of Abdul Qader Abul Fahem from medical negligence; Ashkelon, 1973, which continued for twenty-five days; Ashkelon, 1976, which continued for forty-five days; Junaid Prison, 1983, which lasted for 200 days; Nafha Prison, 1977, which lasted for thirty-two days. An all-out prison hunger strike in 1992 involved 7,000 prisoners for seventeen days; and two other hunger strikes in 1994 and 1996.

Actually, the first hunger strike by Palestinian women was in solidarity with male prisoners in 1996. Women from Rafah and Khan Younis learned that their husbands and brothers were mistreated and ruthlessly punished in Gaza central prison. They moved in groups to the prison to see their menfolk and the wardens viciously drove them back when they tried to gain entry. Israeli soldiers retaliated with live rounds, killing three women and wounding thirteen others.

In response, a hundred women staged a hunger striker in Jerusalem's Holy Sepulchre Church for two nights and three days to protest against the harsh treatment and torture of their men, the notorious, horrible prison conditions, as well as the Israeli occupation as a whole.

Ill-treatment and the threat of rape are commonplace in the Palestinian prison experience. Qahra AlSaddi, a mother and a former political prisoner, who was assaulted, was told that her ten- and sixteen-year-old daughters had been arrested and would be raped unless she complied. Another female political prisoner Issam Abdelhadi's daughter was threatened with rape by her interrogators who beat her with a whip. Muna Qaidan, imprisoned in 1999, was so tortured and humiliated that she lost almost half of her weight. She went on several hunger strikes – in 1999, for thirty-seven days. She was re-imprisoned in 2007 for twenty-one days. In 2014, she was again imprisoned, joined a mass hunger strike and was released after twenty-eight days.

Shireen Issawi, a human rights lawyer, was detained no less than five times, the last of which was in 2014. She went on several hunger strikes to protest the dehumanizing prison conditions. She always demanded her freedom because she was imprisoned with no charge nor trial yet she spent around forty-three months in prison before she was set free.

Palestinian political prisoners, like their fellow Irish political prisoners, practiced a strategy of *Sumud* – steadfastness and a capacity to endure woe and suffering. Hunger striker Terence MacSwiney, who died in Brixton Prison in 1920, put it this way: "It is not those who can inflict the most, but those that can endure the most who will triumph in the end!"

Our prisoners never succumbed to the will of their jailers, oppressors or occupiers notwithstanding the difficult and unbearably dehumanizing and repressive prison conditions. Political prisoners are in the vanguard of defending a just and noble cause in the face of brutal occupation and colonisation.

In apartheid Israeli prisons Palestinian detainees use various creative techniques to abort the machinations and plans of jailers and they continue their struggle through non-violence. They turn their cells and cages into educational hubs, reading and educating themselves, and learning languages, especially English and Hebrew to broaden their knowledge, to equip themselves with the necessary tools of how to deal with their jailers and how to understand the outside world.

Palestinian prisoners – like Irish republican prisoners during the Irish peace process – played a vital role in formulating a political document that unified the different political views of the Palestinian factions, particularly Fatah and Hamas, regarding the Palestinian struggle for freedom adopted by the Palestinian national movement. The document is of paramount importance because it was unanimously accepted by the Palestinian national movement's leadership.

In 1981, Ireland lost ten hunger strikers, including the iconic hero, freedom fighter and poet, Bobby Sands whose name echoes across time and transcends all borders. Sands inspires the Palestinian resistance movement and its political prisoners in Israeli jails who consider Bobby a great role model who willingly sacrificed his life for his country.

Like Sands, a number of Palestinian hunger strikers gave their lives willingly for Palestine. The Palestinian people regard the Irish struggle for freedom with admiration, appreciation and respect. The paradigm of the Irish struggle has been inspiring for Palestinian political prisoners who followed the strategy of *Sumud* to the end.

An example of this is Maher AlAkhras – a father of six children – who, facing unjustifiably frequent administrative detention by the Israeli authorities, went on a hunger strike for freedom or death. His battle continued for well over 103 days, living only on salt and water. The Israeli Prison Service (IPS) tried several times to make him stop his hunger strike by making false promises, but he was determined to achieve his goal and continued fasting despite the medical negligence. He was motivated by the justness and justice of his cause, declaring in simple and clear words that it was a matter of freedom or death. He was ready to give his life not only for his own freedom, but also for the freedom of his own people, forcing his captors and jailers to release him in November 2020. The Israeli prison authorities failed to break him, the same as the British prison authorities failed totally to break the will of Bobby Sands and his eleven comrades, including Michael Gaughan (1974) and Frank Stagg (1976) who died in English jails.

The oppressors and jailers and interrogators in the prisons of Belfast, Armagh, Portlaoise, Long Kesh, or the Israeli jails of Nafha, Junaid, Negev or Ashkelon, used the same methods of torture against political prisoners. The Israeli jailers learned those methods from their British masters – for what is administrative detention but another name for internment without trial?

Many Palestinian political prisoners were killed in prison or died shortly after they were released because of mistreatment and medical negligence. Today, there are well over 4,500 Palestinian prisoners in Israeli jails, including forty women and 150 children. Some 700 of these prisoners have been sentenced to more than twenty years, thirty prisoners have been sentenced to more than twenty-five years, and fourteen prisoners have been sentenced to more than thirty years in prison.

Kareem Younis and Nael Al Bargouthi have been imprisoned since the 1980s. Some 250 Palestinian prisoners have died in prisons since the 1967 occupation of the West Bank and the Gaza Strip. Six hunger strikers were martyred in Israeli jails: AbdelKader AbulFahem, Rasim Mohammed Halwa, Ali Shehada Al Jaafari, Ishak Maragha and Hussien Obiedat, and Anis Doleh. (Addameer).

It is no exaggeration to say and rightly so, that the whole Palestinian people live in a concentration camp. This is the opinion of the Israeli historian Ilan Pappe who elaborated and detailed this very concept in his book, *The Biggest Prison on Earth: A History of the Occupied Territories* (2019). He argues rather convincingly that the occupied territories are the world largest mega-prison. He is of the opinion that Gaza is a maximum security prison and the West Bank is an open air prison. Pappe says the Israeli government offered both versions of the mega-prison to the people of the West Bank and the Gaza Strip. One was an open-air Panopticon prison, the other a maximum security one. If they did not accept the former, they would get the other. This is the inhuman and merciless reality where the Palestinian people "are incarcerated in the biggest ever human prison witnessed in modern history."

Pappe harshly criticizes the Israelis who oppress the Palestinians and ridicules the western officials who condone and praise the Israelis despite their crimes against the Palestinian people. The Israelis, he says, who either support or who do not object to the oppression, are still hailed in the western world as champions of peace and humanity, endowed with an endless stream of undeserved prizes and awards. That said, there are very few really evil people in modern human history, but there are quite a few evil systems. The mega-prison of Palestine is one of them.

I couldn't conclude this introduction, which reflects a shared struggle, without expressing my admiration to the various sectors of the Irish people north and south who never failed to expressed solidarity and show sympathy and support with the Palestinian people, caged as a whole or individually in solitary confinement. Here, one cannot but mention the legendary hunger strike leader Bobby Sands and his comrades.

The Palestinian people are really thankful to the Irish people for the fraternal support they have always been receiving.

Being an activist since my days as a student in UCD and TCD in the 1980s, I feel it is a great honour and noble duty to wholeheartedly thank the Irish people for their great solidarity. I witness that sentiment wherever I go, be it on the streets of Dublin, the precincts of the Dáil, the Senate, the university campuses, trade unions halls, including Liberty Hall. I find it in most of the political parties. One should here be proud of the supportive role of Sinn Féin, People before Profit, the Greens, the Workers Party and the Communist Party. It is there among the Union Students of Ireland, Trade Unions, women activist groups, art organisations and those in other civil society groups.

I must single out for special mention the work of the various solidarity organisations, especially the indefatigable Ireland Palestine Solidarity Campaign, the IPSC. It organises weekly stands in front of the GPO in Dublin and other cities in support of the Palestinian struggle for freedom, justice, self-determination and independence, and highlights ongoing Israeli outrages and human rights abuses.

In my capacity as the international spokesperson of the great March of Return I am grateful to Senator, singer and activist Frances Black for her Occupied Territories Bill which calls for the boycotting of Israeli products grown in settlements stolen from the Palestinian people. I have no doubt that the enormous support from the Irish people for the Palestinian struggle is, at root, motivated by the anti-colonial instinct which saw Ireland's long struggle for its own freedom.

I feel deeply indebted and grateful to the people of Free Derry. In 2019, I was the guest speaker at an event on the anniversary of Bloody Sunday and received an overwhelming welcome. It was during that occasion that I was lucky to have met and cemented a fraternal and friendly relationship with Danny Morrison, a former political prisoner, activist, author and leader, who introduced me to the audience and interviewed me about the Great March of Return protests. As we share the struggle in general, we share now this introduction to these testimonies from former hunger strikers. This shared struggle is destined to be victorious: justice will undoubtedly and certainly defeat injustice and Palestine will be free and Ireland will be free and united.

> *My home land is not a bundle of tales*
> *Nor is it a memory*
> *This land is the skin covering my bones*
> *And my heart vibrates like a bee*
> *Over its grass*
> **~ Mahmoud Darwish**

Asad Abu Shark
Palestinian-Irish academic
Dublin, May 2021

Asad Abu Shark is a Palestinian-Irish academic, living in Dublin, whose family after being ethnically cleansed from the city of Askelon by Zionist gangs, lived in a refugee camp in Rafah. He is the International Spokesperson of the Great March of Return.

Danny Morrison

IN 1920 a young Ho Chi Minh, future President of Vietnam, was working in a London hotel. In Brixton Prison, across the city, a man was dying on hunger strike. It was making world news and Ho Chi Minh followed the story closely. Terence MacSwiney was the Lord Mayor of Cork and a member of the IRA. A few months earlier, British soldiers had stormed his City Hall office and arrested him. He was charged with possession of seditious documents. His trial, by military court-martial, lasted two minutes. He was sentenced to two years and transferred to an English jail.

When MacSwiney died on hunger strike after seventy-four days, Ho Chi Minh wrote to his mother: "A nation which has such citizens will never surrender."

Nelson Mandela recalled that the code word on Robben Island for the ANC hunger strikes was 'Sands'.

When Marwan Barghouti, intifada leader, went on hunger strike he said that he drew inspiration from Bobby Sands and his comrades.

We Irish adapted our republicanism from the American War of Independence and the French Revolution. It was further developed over decades in response to landlordism, industrial exploitation, sectarian discrimination. But a major component of our republicanism is our internationalism.

To be a revolutionary you must be an internationalist. You must support 'the wretched of the earth' in their struggles. We are all one.

Today, in the 21st century, right before our eyes, the Palestinian people are being destroyed by one of the cruellest and most cynical regimes in the Middle East, Israel, a state that is bankrolled by the US government and which flagrantly has breached every UN Resolution since December 1948, including Resolution 194 which supports the right of Palestinian refugees who fled or were expelled to return to their homes. Since 1967 Israel refuses to withdraw from the territories it then occupied, continues to conquer, to build settlements, ghettoising the Palestinians and rendering impossible any viable Palestinian state.

The Palestinians, relying first and foremost on their own strength, know that they can rely upon the support of Irish republicans because we have both experienced the incredible suffering and pain associated with occupation. It is an honour to have worked on this book with Asad, Norma, Yousef and Low, which combines into one the story of two prison struggles and the desperate use of the hunger strike by men and women to highlight injustice and oppression.

Irish republicans when imprisoned have always refused to be treated as criminals. They defended their own integrity and the integrity of their struggle by refusing to conform unless they were recognised as political prisoners or prisoners of war.

The first Irish hunger striker to die was Thomas Ashe in 1917; the last was Mickey Devine in 1981. In total, twenty-three prisoners died; twelve during our last phase of armed conflict.

A hunger strike in 1972 in Belfast Prison forced the British government to recognise political status before there were any deaths. But four years later the British reneged on this arrangement. Convicted prisoners were stripped of their clothes and thrown into cells in the H-Blocks of Long Kesh where they wore only a blanket to cover their nakedness. The prisoners lived in inhuman conditions for years, deprived of basic rights. They were regularly beaten and hosed down.

In 1981 Bobby Sands began a hunger strike for the restoration of political status. The strike lasted for seven months and ten prisoners died – two of whom, Bobby Sands and Kieran Doherty, were elected to the British and Irish parliaments, respectively. Earlier, two republican prisoners, Frank Stagg and Michael Gaughan, had died on hunger strike in England, demanding to be repatriated to jails closer to the families.

Prisoners' families formed Relatives Action Committees and a National H-Block/Armagh Committee to campaign on their behalf. Leading members of this committee were assassinated by loyalists/British agents. During the 1981 hunger strike the British army and the RUC provoked riots and ruthlessly attacked protesters and mourners. They killed men, women and children with live rounds and with plastic bullets, including fourteen-year-old Julie Livingstone, eleven-year-old Carol Ann Kelly and mother-of-three Nora McCabe. Hundreds more were hospitalised with serious injuries. In Belfast alone, 30,000 plastic bullets were fired.

After the hunger strike the prisoners eventually won all their demands.

After the hunger strike Sinn Féin developed an election strategy, building on Bobby Sands' winning a seat in the British parliament.

In the 1990s we also entered into a peace process which resulted in many gains for the struggle, but not yet for the complete end of British interference in Irish affairs. Prisoners were given early release and many of them – former blanket men, surviving hunger strikers and escapees – went on to become Sinn Féin negotiators and in impressive numbers were elected to office at council level, to the northern Assembly, the Dáil and Westminster.

Forty years after the deaths of the ten H-Block prisoners their sacrifice and that of their comrades continue to have an impact in Ireland and further afield.

Certainly the hunger strike's most initial tangible effects were to re-energise and increase support for the Republican Movement and the struggle.

Today, our morale is buoyant. In all likelihood Sinn Féin (currently in coalition government in the North) will also be the lead party in the next government in the Republic of Ireland where it will then ensure that its 2014 motion calling for the recognition of the State of Palestine will be acted upon.

The cause of Palestine is the cause of Ireland.

The cause of Ireland is the cause of Palestine!

Danny Morrison
Belfast, May 2021

Danny Morrison, a former prisoner and former Director of Publicity for Sinn Féin, is the secretary of the Bobby Sands Trust. He is the author of several books and plays.

Excerpts from the H-Block Trilogy

And who are we but mortal men
Who burn in others' hate,
And slump beneath the murderous load
Of torture's gruelling weight.
But though we slump we do not fall
And endless is our fate.

We do not wear the guilty stare
Of those who bear a crime,
Nor do we don that badge of wrong
To tramp the penal line.
So men endure a pit of sewer
For freedom of the mind.

Beneath the sky men live and die
For man must die from birth.
And some never see the flower or tree
Or know their lovely worth,
But in the gloom of prison tomb
Men crave for Mother earth.

We fought back tears and scorned our fears
And cast aside our pain
And to our doors we stood in scores
To conquer their black fame
For loud and high we sang our cry
'A Nation Once Again!'

Bobby Sands
Bobby died after sixty-six days on hunger strike, 5 May, 1981

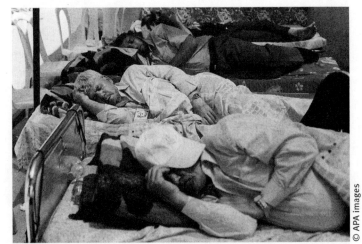

Palestinians including former prisoners on hunger strike in solidarity with Palestinian hunger strikers in Israeli jails.

The Stories

A Life Between Two Deaths

Mohammed Alian
Palestine

I SAT down on an old wooden bench and took up a book, in my other hand I held a glass of water from which I had a sip. The book didn't interest me, I felt my memory calling me elsewhere on that hot July day.

In a paragraph my eyes fell on the word 'Ali'. I saw it as if it was carved onto the page. At once the name took me to the heart of pain.

That name had been with me through the hardest of times.

My hands shook and forced me to put the glass of water down.

Your name Ali, compelled me to rise and look to the horizon where I saw heaven and a mountain of memories, that brought me back thirty years to my most painful memory ever.

It was a very hot day in the summer of 1982 when I was a prisoner serving a life sentence. Those years, taken from me, weigh as heavy on my mind as the tragedy of our lost homeland.

I was a young man in my 30s, in what were supposed to be the best and brightest years of my life, confined to spending them in the dark hell of an Israeli prison.

The cell was too narrow for my dreams and imagination.

In a corner of the prison, which I called home, I found a quiet place to relive my dreams. My mother's face and the laughter of the children in our neighbourhood, came back to me.

Those dreams of laughter were shattered and my beautiful mother's face faded away with the sound of Israeli soldiers stomping their way to our cell.

We thought it was just another inspection, but they tied us up, from our feet to our necks, prevented us from speaking and took us in a rickety truck to Nafha, a new prison in the desert.

This was just the beginning of our hell.

There were no windows in the cells, even if our view of the world was a desert, it would have been something to look at.

We were locked-up behind heavy iron doors and forced to share our cells with reptiles, who ran on our beds and ate from our dishes.

We quickly decided to end the torment, we didn't care about what we might lose, we wanted to end this injustice or at least have a less painful punishment.

This is the horror of life in an Israeli prison.

Fifty prisoners started a hunger strike, we wanted a better life. We were clinging to hope and praying for a better future. We paid a very heavy price, but from the beginning we preferred death to living like this.

Only then did I realise, that you Ali, were the winner among us.

With the start of the strike the Israeli Prison Service (IPS) came down hard on us.

In our minds the prison became our cemetery.

Our unity was the light that lit our darkness and led us to victory.

The number of prisoners who went on hunger strike reached one hundred and twenty. We declared that we would only drink water, which became our only, lonely companion.

We completed a month of an historic hunger strike.

Ali, if I could have seen what would happen: I would have wished it had been me. The soldiers broke into our cell and chained my hands to yours; you would smile despite your weakness and with your undernourished body, whisper to me, "I didn't lose too much of my weight in this strike." I would smile back at you as we waited together.

They eventually tied up all the prisoners and took us on a torturous journey to Ramleh Prison, where history was written with blood.

Our emaciated bodies were riddled with pain while the soldiers' only goal was to stop this strike.

We vowed to make their efforts worthless.

The beatings, tortures, hangings and abuse just strengthened our resolve to continue. Frequent rounds of torture exhausted us.

We would be stretched on the ground most of the time, our bodies and souls would scream equally in pain.

They began bringing pairs of prisoners bound together to the prison's clinic. We foolishly thought that mercy had found its way in to their hearts, until we heard the screams.

The prisoners resisted this hell and succeeded in defying the injustice.

We didn't know what was going on until our turn came.

Ali, you were racing to get past me as if you wanted to be first in line to challenge the jailer.

He was taking us to that dark room and it seemed you were rushing to your fate with your head held high and with the dignity that will never diminish in my mind.

I saw you chained and resisting their hatred as they forced a plastic tube filled with water and salt into your mouth, causing you to vomit a pool of blood.

You still refused to surrender. I called your name, to give you strength. I saw your sad, shackled body surrounded by a pool of blood but you still insisted on continuing your hunger strike.

The screams after those tubes were forced down our throats broke the silence in the prison that day.

They took you to another room, we heard your screams of pain. I saw a trail of blood leading to the place where they took you.

They put me in a nearby cell with some other prisoners where we could hear your screams ring out from the top of your lungs. Oh, how I needed to see your smile to remove the heavy pain from my heart.

I saw you in my dreams, falling asleep in your mother's lap, like a baby. Your voice weakened and no matter how much I strained I could no longer hear it.

We knocked in vain repeatedly on the cell door begging for a word from you but all I could hear was the beating of my heart and the feet of the soldiers around you.

They soon declared you dead.

I saw you free Ali, for the first time, not shackled with pain. I saw you leaving injustice, oppression and prison behind.

Ali, you lived with dignity and left with it.

In your screams, before your martyrdom, you declared our protest a victory. Now, still, you bring us hope.

In memory of hunger strikers Ali al-Jaafari and Rasim Halawa. ■

Mohammed Alian is a 63-year-old former Palestinian political prisoner who is married with four children. He works as a lawyer. He spent ten years in Israeli jails and was released as part of Jibril Prisoner Swap Agreement in 1985. He lives in Jerusalem.

'For You, Frank'

George Stagg
Ireland

FRANK Stagg (pictured above) died on hunger strike in an English jail in February 1976, less than twenty months after the death on hunger strike of his fellow Mayo man and comrade, Michael Gaughan.

Frank's brother, George, tells the incredible story of how Frank's body was hijacked on the orders of a Fine Gael/Labour coalition government and entombed beneath four tonnes of concrete in an unmarked grave, all to deny him his dying wish to be buried beside Michael Gaughan.

My father had been in the old IRA and had been arrested in the Tan War and the Civil War. In fact, as a young girl my mother saw him being arrested by the Tans and being marched over to the barracks in Hollymount and that's when she first took a shine to him! My brother Frank was the seventh of thirteen children. He had a confident air about himself and would protect us younger ones in school or in football games etc., against any bullying, or the like. He was a very honest man, wouldn't tell you a lie. I looked up to him and I'd have followed him anywhere – which in the end, I had to.

He was a good singer and some of the songs he sang included ones about the characters in Hollymount, and the Toormakeady ambush. He was also an outstanding handballer at which he won Mayo and Connaught championships. He was a top-class club footballer as well. The land around Robeen, the home place, was not bad, but the holdings were very small, about fifteen to thirty acres per family. Many people were forced to emigrate and so Frank left for England in 1960 when he was eighteen. He worked as a construction worker, then on the buses in Coventry and later married a fellow Mayo woman, Bridie Armstrong.

When the troubles broke out in the Six Counties Frank felt he had to do something for the nationalist people. He had become involved with Sinn Féin, fund-raising, selling ballot tickets, and then he joined an IRA unit in Coventry. He and five others were arrested in a police swoop in 1973 and were charged with conspiracy to cause explosions. He was sentenced to ten years but for refusing to do penal work he spent many long periods in solitary confinement and was on hunger strike on several occasions with similar demands each time – he wanted to be treated as a political prisoner and repatriated to a prison in the Six Counties. He also demanded that his family not be strip-searched on visits. My mother, Mary, in her seventies, was frequently strip-searched and had to run the gauntlet of English National Front protesters outside the prison, screaming abuse into her face. I approached the Irish government to intervene with the British Home Secretary to provide my mother with some protection. I met Garret Fitzgerald. He was very arrogant and dismissive and wanted to lecture me about how Fine Gael dealt with hunger strikers themselves. I got up and said, "I don't want lectures, I want protection for my mother."

Two years before Frank's arrest, Michael Gaughan from Ballina, who was in the London IRA, had been sentenced to seven years for a bank raid. In prison he encountered the Kray twins, East End gangsters, who were bullying a number of Jamaican prisoners. Michael defended the Jamaicans, faced up to the Krays telling them that he had the IRA behind him. They soon backed off!

It was in Parkhurst Prison that Frank met Michael and they became close friends and comrades.

Another group of IRA prisoners from Belfast, including the Price sisters, Hugh Feeney and Gerry Kelly, had begun a hunger strike demanding that they be repatriated closer to home in Ireland to serve their sentences where prisoners had political status. Frank and Michael joined them on hunger strike.

The prisoners were force-fed, every three days over a period of more than two hundred days. Six or seven burly warders would move your bed into the middle of the cell, surround you, force your head back, clamp your mouth with a block of wood and force a tube down your throat and into your stomach. The night before Michael died in Parkhurst in June 1974 the warders had force-fed him, cutting his throat and loosening his teeth. He had no way of protesting or alerting them. Food, or gruel, had been lodged in his lungs. Frank went into see him and Michael said, "I'm dying. They've clogged my lungs."

When Michael's body was brought back to Dublin it lay in state in a Franciscan church where thousands filed past it. During the funeral procession from Dublin to Ballina thousands upon thousands of people lined the streets in all the towns to pay their respects. The Fine Gael/Labor coalition government was furious.

Michael was buried with full IRA military honours in Leigue Cemetery in Ballina.

The hunger strike ended two weeks later after assurances were given that the prisoners would be moved to jails in the Six Counties. But when the four Belfast prisoners were eventually transferred, Frank was not included. Authorities went back on their word. Instead, they moved him to another jail where he began his protest all over again. They said that Frank was not a native of the North but of the South of Ireland, so Frank went back on hunger strike again, his fourth in two years. This time he declared that he would not come off hunger strike until he had arrived at a prison in the North.

I visited him in Wakefield a number of times — one of those old, cold Victorian prisons. My sister, Martha, recalls Frank telling my mother that the warders were mocking him about a letter she (Martha) had written, begging him to come off and saying she didn't want him to die. She was very upset and apologised to Frank on the next visit. My mother told the family that the best way of dealing with differences of opinion is that we support Frank. We hadn't come through what he had suffered and was suffering.

Frank let it be known that in the event of his death he wanted to be buried with military honours and he wanted to be buried in the same grave as his comrade Michael Gaughan. He signed a codicil to his will to that effect a few days before he died. He had hoped that this would pressure the Dublin government — who didn't want another huge funeral like Michael's – to intervene with the British and get them to compromise. Instead, the Irish government asked the British government not to hand his body over to the Republican Movement.

I'm looking at the codicil which Frank wrote and signed:

"I, Frank Stagg, give all authority to the Provisional Movement to make statements on my behalf. I make this request of my own free will.

"Derek Highstead is to take full charge of my funeral arrangements.

"I want full military honours.

"I leave the route of the funeral to be arranged by the Republican Movement.

"My demands are the same as always.

"I request a visit from a doctor named by me.

"F. Stagg. 7/2/1976. Wakefield Prison."

My mother and Bridie were with Frank in Wakefield Prison when he died in his cell at 6.20am, on 12 February, 1976. He had been sixty-two days on hunger strike. He was thirty-four. About eight o'clock in the morning I was in my car when I heard the news of his death on the radio. That's how I found out he was dead. I stopped the car, pulled in, and I just sat and thought about him for a while. He was at peace then, because he had gone through some torture.

Make no mistake, Frank did not want to die, he wanted to live. It was now our duty to honour his last wishes to the letter, and unite around him as Mam had said. But that is not how it turned out. Following the inquest and just before the release of his body we had a family meeting in my sister's house in Coventry to finalise arrangements for the removal of Frank's coffin to Ireland. Bridie, Frank's widow, was distraught but had been content that, as per Frank's final written wishes, Derek Highstead and myself would look after all the funeral arrangements. A relative of Bridie's, a priest, who had not supported Frank in any way or even, to my knowledge, up to that point had not shown or expressed any interest in Frank's welfare or situation, suddenly appeared on the scene for the first time since Frank's arrest and began to assert himself. He and my brother Emmet, who would later become a Labour Party TD (a member of the Irish parliament), and who also had not been a supporter of Frank's republicanism, began to insist on a private funeral, which in reality, was the funeral best suited to the Irish government but which also, knowingly, denied Frank's final wish. My mother and all the other siblings wanted to abide by Frank's will, that he be given the republican funeral his dying wish had requested and which he had arranged with his comrades.

It was a tense and extremely distressful time for us all – leading to bitterness and division which has only receded with the passage of time. Meantime, the British police asked for a meeting with myself and Derek at which they insisted that the coffin could only be flown to Ireland in a cargo plane, instead of the hold of a passenger plane with all family mourners on board, as is normal procedure, and as Derek and myself had booked earlier. Now only one member of the family was to be allowed to accompany the coffin and, after consultation with Bridie and the family, it was agreed that should be myself. There were only three seats at the back of the cargo plane, and when I boarded two of the seats were already occupied by two men. The middle seat was free and I sat in it. Nobody spoke. One of the men produced the *Irish Independent* from his pocket and proceeded to read it. Half-way through the flight he put the paper down and I asked him if I could have a read of it. I wanted to see what they were saying about Frank. When we landed and started taxiing towards the terminal, I couldn't reconcile whereabouts we were in Dublin Airport. I said to one of the men, "What part of Dublin Airport is this? "Dublin? This is Shannon." The other one stood up, produced a badge from his pocket and said, "Irish Special Branch. You are under arrest." "What did I do?" I asked.

"I don't have to give you any more information, you are under arrest."

The pilot came down the plane and he looked at me with a sympathetic gaze. I later learnt that when the plane entered Irish airspace, he was ordered by the government to divert to Shannon and refused the instruction. The Department of Justice was forced to hurriedly issue a National Security Alert with which the pilot had to comply.

I was bundled into a police car and taken to Ennis, about sixteen miles away, and was put in a cell. Then I was brought into another room and questioned about whether I had any involvement in "any oul organisation." Those were their actual words. I said, "No. But I'm a member of the Labor Party," which I was back then. After about an hour I was released without charge. A sympathetic taxi driver from Ennis drove me back to Shannon Airport mortuary but I was locked out by Gardaí. I was soon joined outside the morgue by that redoubtable local republican and Derry native, Brigid Makowski, who offered empathy, tea, sandwiches and, if needed, money. Brigid is since sadly deceased, RIP. Meanwhile, my elderly mother and other members of our family were waiting anxiously at Dublin airport, awaiting our arrival, and didn't know what was going on. When they learnt that Frank's remains were in Shannon they immediately set out for there and brought down my car. Some of us kept vigil in my car outside the morgue from where we could see a small blurred image of the corner of the coffin through a frosted window. But at about three in the morning we were approached by a Garda superintendent who said, "We need that car to move away." I told him I wasn't moving. Next thing, about fifteen guards got around the car, lifted it off the ground and moved it back about twenty metres to a place from where we could no longer see the coffin. Shortly afterwards three figures in full-cover white boiler suits entered the morgue. They emerged about two hours later carrying several stainless-steel type canisters and containers.

On Friday morning the mortuary was surrounded by armed troops. An Air Corps army helicopter landed and we saw Gardaí shoulder Frank's coffin to the helicopter. When we tried to follow them about a hundred guards blocked our way. We were shouting and screaming that we were prevented from seeing our brother. Everybody was in tears. I pointed my finger at a Superintendent and demanded to know where they were taking Frank. He refused to answer. I said, "I'm telling you now, I promise you. A day will come and I'll have him back. And I promise you that."

The helicopter was flown to our local church in Robeen which was surrounded by heavily armed troops and police and an armoured car. All roads to the church were blocked by checkpoints. Guards kept a watch on his coffin through the night and the church was lit up by arc lights from the road and fields.

Our distraught family was faced with a major dilemma. The state had possession of Frank's body. Do we take part in this 'state' operation, or not? Mam and the vast majority of us stayed away. Our Veronica, a true hard-nosed republican who supported Frank at all times, and who died herself shortly afterwards, went to the funeral. She told me some months after the funeral, "I just could not envisage a situation where Frank would be buried and I would not be there."

Looking back on it now, with all the tension and mixed emotions of that time, I'm completely at peace with the fact that every member of the family mourned Frank in their own way and in the way that they felt was right.

After Mass his coffin was placed in a hearse, followed by ten armoured cars, trucks and lorries and taken in haste to Ballina through backroads. Minister of Justice Patrick Cooney had ordered that Frank be buried about seventy yards from the Republican Plot in an empty part of Leigue Cemetery.

The following day the Republican Movement organised a march through Ballina. About twenty thousand people gathered. The Gardaí tried to stop us from getting into the cemetery but they relented under weight of numbers. When the IRA fired a volley of shots over the grave, the police and army attacked and scuffles broke out. Many people were injured in the baton charge and the discharge of rubber bullets by the army.

The Guards put on a 24-hour watch on the grave – five Gardaí in three cars and the Branch stationed in a builder's hut, a few yards away. Anyone who visited the grave was photographed.

My mother had yet to visit the grave so I took her there the following week. Special Branch officers came out of the hut and took photographs of her as she knelt and prayed. I thought it was the most heartless thing I'd ever seen.

The caretaker of the cemetery was Gerry Ginty, who happened also to be a Sinn Féin councillor. His mother, Jane, also worked in admin, selling lots, etc. I asked Gerry one day, out of the blue, "By the way, who bought that grave, who paid for it?" He said, nobody. I asked could I buy it. I took out my cheque book to pay three pounds. "How much are you going to give me?" Said Jane. I said, "Three pounds." "No," she said. "Give me a fiver. For a fiver you can get 'a double'. That grave and the one next to it." "Why?" I asked. And she said, "In case you ever have to dig down." So, I bought both.

I got a headstone erected on the empty plot which read, "Here in a grave dug by government agents lies the body of Vol. Proinsias Stagg. His will required that he be buried in the Republican Plot alongside his comrade in the IRA Vol. M. Gaughan. Having died on hunger strike in an English jail his body was stolen and defiled by the pro-British Dublin government of the day. The truth for which he lived will blossom when his remains are reburied with the Republicans of Mayo. Erected by his Comrades and family."

The Guards maintained a round-the-clock watch on the grave. But after about a year they realised that it was a waste of garda time and resources. So, instead of the vigil they poured concrete on top of the grave. We estimated that they must have used about four tonnes.

That summer, 1977, I got a call from Gerry Ginty, who had already been hatching a plan for the removal of Frank. He said, "We can do this!"

We didn't know if the concrete went down the sides also, entombing the coffin and making it virtually impossible to break into the grave from the side without using machinery, which would attract attention. We reckoned we needed six trustworthy people in total for the operation. Gerry and I made two. Gerry got one other, Con Ryan, and I got the other three — my brother-in-law Jimmy Doyle, Sean Cumiskey from Trim, and Paul Stanley from Kildare.

Gerry chose the night carefully, 5 November, a night when there was no moon, was very dark, but, unfortunately, a bitterly cold night, with continuous driving rain. We had two lookouts – one up the town, and the other down at the gates of the graveyard. Four of us would carry out the digging. Two on, two off. We made good progress but we were soon soaked through to the skin. There was hardly anyone out and about on a night like this but at one stage the blue light of a garda patrol car was flashing down near the gates and we thought we were gone. We later learnt that the driver stopped to offer a lift to a rain-drenched pedestrian. Once or twice headlights from cars leaving a nearby house swept across the cemetery and forced us to duck.

When we had dug about four foot down a massive rock materialised, about five foot in diameter and it must have weighed about a quarter of a ton. We thought: this is it; we're not going to be able to get this out. But Gerry said to keep trying. We sent for the lookout to give us a hand. Two men were down in the hole and we got a rope around it and rolled it up the bank, inch by inch. It was a miracle. After we removed it, we stopped digging down and began to dig sidewise into Frank's grave. Then we discovered there was no concrete down the sides!

It wasn't long afterwards that we struck the wood of the coffin and thankfully it was in fairly good shape. We had quite a bit of trouble getting it to move because it was stuck there by suction. But, again, Gerry was very clever. He just dug little holes over the coffin and to the back of it, until we were able to put the ropes through and gently move it outwards.

I felt very proud. That I was fulfilling a great sense of duty. I was very mindful of the words I said to the superintendent at Shannon. "I'm telling you now, I promise you. A day will come and I'll have him back."

I placed my hands on the coffin and I whispered, "For you, Frank. We're doing this for you, Frank."

We placed the coffin on a sheet of plywood – which Gerry had 'carelessly' (!) left lying around a few days earlier after closing another grave – in case Frank's coffin would disintegrate while being moved. We carried it down to the Republican Plot and within a short time we had Frank's remains re-interred beside his comrade Michael Gaughan. We then said a prayer and then we saluted. We withdrew from the graveyard, it was not yet dawn, and each went his own way. I got in the car and headed back home.

Later, I rang my mother to tell her it was done, to listen out for the news, and she cried and she thanked me.

The RTE newsroom was tipped off and ran the story about the re-interment of Frank Stagg. Special Branch visited Gerry Ginty and asked him to accompany them to the cemetery. When they got there hundreds of people had gathered around the plot. One old man said, "Gerry, you did a great job last night." Even the detectives smiled at the jibe. No one was ever charged. Frank Stagg's dying wishes had been honoured. ■

George Stagg (b. 1948) came from a staunch republican family in County Mayo. His father was an IRA intelligence officer in the South Mayo Brigade (1919-1922) and in the civil war was shot and imprisoned by the Free State government. His mother's uncle died in action after an ambush against British forces in 1920. Frank and George were very close. George is a lifelong republican and an activist to this day, supporting the cause of freedom for which Frank gave his life.

This story has been published earlier and is being published in this book with the kind permission of the author and the publisher, Elsinor Verlag.

Drowning in My Memories

Ismaat Mansour
Palestine

AFTER finishing work, I strolled back to my beautiful home, in the shimmering sunlight. A soft breeze brushed my face, which brought short relief from the anguish that was to come in my mind.

My joy rose as children played before me using a bottle as a ball, but suddenly, the sound of their toy in my day dream, brought me back with a bang to the sound of a water bottle being passed around by twenty hunger strikers in a dark cell some years ago.

I had been on hunger strike along with other inmates in an Israeli Occupiers' Prison.

Water was all we had whenever we were about to fall unconscious or suffered nausea.

Back then, it wasn't easy being a member of a hunger strike's leadership group, even when our demands were clear and unambiguous, like the need to move prisoners out of death cells (isolation cells) and getting permission for family visits for a prisoner's family from the Gaza Strip.

To be in charge of a hunger strike was a great responsibility, all I worried about was the fate of the strikers and the desire of the hungry souls for freedom, not food.

After twenty days without food the prison's administration used vile strategies to torture us, but these actions only increased our belief that we were in the right and had chosen the correct path to achieve out demands.

I took part in discussions with the prison authorities, who attempted to offer us limited concessions which despite our weakness and hunger we clearly said 'no' to and returned to our cells with patience, their show of weakness gave us a ray of hope to hang on to.

Going back to those hunger strike days of 2012, I recalled that our faces were pale and our bodies were weak, our blood seemed lost under our skins but we did not despair.

New and harder sanctions aimed to break our determination followed further discussions with prison authorities but this time things had changed, prison authority representatives appealed to us, to try convince prisoners to end the strike.

We felt a little dignity when one of them said, "We will give you everything you want, but stop this crazy thing."

I could not believe what I'd heard and asked him to repeat it several times, until smiles appeared on our faces.

When the hunger strike finally ended, we were happy to tell the prisoners about their victory. Forgetting the pain in my exhausted body, I made my way as swiftly as I could to my fellow prisoners in Ofer Prison to tell them the good news.

I didn't have to speak, the expression on my face said it all. On realising what it meant there were outpourings of relief from the weak bodies of the brave strikers, howls of joy could be heard throughout the prison.

They hugged each other, while remembering the long days of hunger and pain they had bravely suffered together.

The proud hunger strikers, by their efforts had struck a blow in the battle for humanitarian rights in the harsh conditions of an Israeli occupation prison. ∎

Ismaat Mansour is a 45-year-old former Palestinian political prisoner who spent twenty years in Israeli jails and was released in August 2013. He lives in Ramallah in the West Bank.

Shadowed Dreams

Adeeb Mafarja
Palestine

H E raised his hands and smiling waved at me. His life was quiet and peaceful. No bullets had scarred his face, leaving his features smooth and gentle. He moved slowly away from me, and in my dream called my name, I answered, "Mohammed, Mohammed."

I repeated it several times until I felt a burn in my throat that awoke me. I looked around but could not find him.

There were only four walls, choking me and blocking the fresh air. My eyes found the cell floor, which was as hard as our lives, and a heavy door, in the prison in which we were caged.

If only I could live those times again before we were imprisoned.

My deepest wish is to meet you again brother, before

your martyrdom Mohammed, to take in all meanings of your smile and the scent of jasmine left by your footsteps. I have not been able to look at pictures of you since your departure, forcing me to resort to dreams of you.

If only I could turn back the clock and meet you before their war machine assassinated you and before your blood was spilled onto the ground, where fields of roses now grow on the mountain that was witness to your heroism.

I rubbed my face and took a drink of cloudy water in a bid to end my thirst. I felt pain in my throat and heard my friend Faud trembling as he tried to rise from his bed, which was only a thin blanket on a dark solid floor.

His beard covered part of his neck; his eyes were full of pain after a month-long hunger strike for freedom. His body told a sad story in itself.

"I saw Mohammed," Faud said, focusing his eyes on a narrow corner of the cell. "He was smiling and waving at me," he added before falling silent. He was trying in vain to remember details of his dream. I put my hand on his shoulder, he looked weak and with tears in his eyes told me of his longing for our Mohammed Assi, his brother and my friend, whose absence had left a wound in our hearts.

Faud got up from his bed, walked to the iron door and kicked it, he was thinking about his martyred brother, more than being angry.

Then he surprised me by asking, "If Mohammed was with us now what would he do?" We shared memories of Mohammed, we laughed over the happy days and wept over our sad loss.

Faud and I decided to go on hunger strike for the freedom we craved, following our placement in administrative detention that stole our lives and shattered our hopes. Our arrest followed the martyrdom of Mohammed. We felt that the strike was the least we could do to honour his memory and that we ought to refuse injustice as he did. Suffering pain and grief, we stayed in the same cell, which was witness to our torment.

The hunger strike made our bodies weak and reflected what we had been through. The jailers tortured us as if we were two birds in a cage, they tried to bring us down using all forms of torture, but failed.

The image of Mohammed stayed with us during the strike providing us with determination and patience in our battle to seek freedom.

We wrote the story of our victory with our resilience, defeating administrative detention after fifty-eight days of hunger strike.

We got out of prison, where longing for Mohammed led us to his grave. There the sweet memories of the three of us, mingled again.

We heard his voice calling us and his face smiling at us from afar. We cried out in joy at the top of our voices, "Mohammed, Mohammed." ∎

Adeeb Mafarja is a 37-year-old former Palestinian prisoner who spent a total of eight years in Israeli jails and was released in November 2016 after going on an open hunger strike for three months to protest his demonstration detention. He was arrested several times before and after his hunger strike, including for seventeen months under administrative detention without charge or a trial.

Four Walls

Akram Al-Rikhawi
Palestine

FOUR walls watched me twenty-four hours a day, observing me. I used to ramble between these walls, composing remnants of memories as if quenching a thirst like a person yearning for water.

I believe nothing is crueller than being a prisoner of your enemy. Nothing is harsher than being chronically ill and incarcerated at the same time. Walls surround you from the inside, so does the pain inside you.

Hardly being able to breath, asthma was killing me. I felt doctors were imprisoning me. How ugly the clinic of Al-Ramle Prison was! I urgently needed medicine. Oh people! Oh world! I cried. My chest felt shattered into pieces.

Asthma was slaughtering me.

I had been suffering from dyspnea, a difficulty in breathing, along with many other ailments since I was first detained in 2004.

I had partially lost my eyesight, had osteoporosis resulting in pains in my bones. All of my illnesses resulted in severe headaches.

It's possible I fear, that some of the prison's Zionist doctors gave me inappropriate medication for asthma.

For many years there have been no serious keeping of international regulations in the prisons of the Israeli occupation.

One Israeli doctor I requested a medical check from said I was fine, not believing him I later had an examination outside the prison and I was diagnosed with having high blood pressure, diabetes and osteoporosis.

It became clear to me that for many years the occupation had been giving me cortisone, a medicine used to treat pain, instead of kenacort, which is used for treating asthma. For nine years I had been taking cortisone, a dangerous medicine I believe when wrongly prescribed.

No one ever cared for my health in those dark, grave-like cells. I felt we were surrounded by beasts, dressed in white.

While the rest of the world regard these people as angels, there they acted like reckless monsters. I felt they lacked humanity and were unscrupulous. Torturing the sick, it seems, was their only joy.

Worrying in my cell, I searched for solutions but there was nothing but pain inside my broken chest.

I decided a hunger strike was my only weapon, I refused food and stopped taking my medication.

"Akram this is a serious decision; will I succeed and the will of the warden be broken," I told myself.

After beginning the strike my body went feeble and my illness increased.

With no food and no medicine to regulate the iron levels in my blood, my emaciated body suffered.

I lost 19kg, my body was weak and my eyes looked tired.

After a while my weight dropped to 49kg.

Suddenly after at least fifty days on hunger strike, officers along with some soldiers entered my prison hospital room.

"You will die here, no one will help you, look at your body, what do you want?" One officer shouted at me.

I told him I wanted the asthma medication, kenacort. The officer smirked and said why not take cortisone and then left my room.

I had to concentrate on my main demand which was obtaining the appropriate medication for asthma.

I vowed to continue my hunger strike and not surrender.

Days passed and negotiations continued. I then decided to insist on achieving my complete freedom, I was sick of pain and suffering, you either die or live with dignity.

I received another setback when I lost the eyesight in my left eye. I believed this was caused by cataract surgery I previously had at the hands of Israeli administration doctors.

After all my agony, I got a little hope; a doctor of the International Organization of Human Rights' insisted my condition was very serious and ordered that I should be given appropriate medicine.

Deep inside I knew he hadn't the power to do anything, as the occupation didn't recognise or care about such international organisations. If they did, things would have been a lot different, neither torture or suffering would have taken place.

On the hundredth and fourth day of hunger strike, I could not walk, talk or see. There were large swellings on all parts of my body.

The very same day, the warden gave in to my demands and granted me freedom. At last I am free... free in Gaza, yet pain still affects me.

Blood pressure, diabetes, asthma and an eye disorder still make my life terrible. ■

Akram Al-Rikhawi is a 48-year-old former Palestinian political prisoner who works as a freelancer. He spent nine years in Israeli jails and was released in 2013. He currently resides in Rafah in the Gaza Strip.

Morning Sighed

Khalil Abu Aram

Morning sighed and the sparrows chittered.
My ears, moved by their hymns, were enraptured.

I wondered, amazed
that small birds fled their nests so early
and scattered.

They roamed the earth, assured
that God is their sustainer, and trusted.
And broke forth, at the dawn, in the east, whilst its rays
glistened,
and the golden threads of its rising disk
penetrated my prison-cell.

As if they were a flash of lightning or a splendid blaze,
from the fervour of burning, irradiated.
Or gleaming shards of crystal by which the deep-black
horizon was illuminated.

They brightened my chamber, and dispersed the darkness
once wrapped around me unsatiated;
carried life into tombs that a planet of prisoners had
overcrowded.

Their crime was a passion for life and homeland,
and their eyes, for freedom and independence, lamented.
For time had handled them roughly,
and the enemy had left them disfigured.

The glare of ultraviolet beams were an incitement to life,
a resurrection overwhelming silence.

Thoughts kindled. In the heart awoke a tenderness,
a yearning, long extinguished.

Khalil Abu Aram, born in Yatta, Hebron, is 53-years-old and has been imprisoned by the Israeli occupation for the last eighteen years. In jail he completed both a BA in Business Administration and a Master's in Regional Studies from Al-Quds Open University. He has also written several monographs on the state of the Palestinian resistance from his unique and highly knowledgeable perspective. As of August 2020, he has been on an open-ended hunger strike, one of many, to protest inhumane prison conditions, breaches of human rights and denial of visitors. He is married and has five children.

A Palestinian on his 30th day of hunger strike holding a poster that calls on people to express solidarity with Palestinian administrative detainees in Israeli jails who are held without charge or trial.

Dicing with Death

Ayman Al-Sharawna
Palestine

A HUNGER strike is a massive game... a dangerous game, and even a deadly gamble in which one could lose one's life.

The protest I undertook can take away your freedom but I vowed that whatever happened, the outcome would not cost me my free will.

The Israeli Occupiers do not recognise laws and agreements that were made to safeguard our basic rights inside prisons.

The greatest fear they faced was that we would die in prison, as it would have been a way for us to achieve our freedom.

They wanted to keep us alive even if it meant dragging us around in wheelchairs. After ten years in prison, I was freed briefly for three months.

Not enough time to get to know new members of my family and friends, let alone stroll through the developed areas of the Hebron and Dura neighbourhoods.

Now once again Israeli soldiers armed to the teeth, broke into my home and hauled me away, even though I had not violated the terms of the deal in which I was released.

As I said my previous prison term lasted ten years and I was scared that the new sentence would be as long.

This time they threw me into Asion Prison, then Ofer and I finally ended up in Ramon Prison.

My legal adviser informed me that the Israeli court wanted to re-sentence me. It is important to say that I was first sentenced to thirty-eight years before the Shalit-Palestinian Prisoners Swap Deal.

After the previous ten years in jail, now an Israeli court was sentencing me to another twenty-eight years. How, I asked myself, could I cope with such a long time locked behind bars? I decided a hunger strike was the only option open to me.

I knew it wasn't a game; I could lose my life or could end up ill and suffer in agony for the rest of my life.

At first after the decision to stop taking food, the time passed quickly but after a hundred days hunger is seemingly endless.

Hunger became not as much as a challenge but a battle that grew violently between me and my jailers.

They used criminal and barbaric ways just to make me quit.

My health was deteriorating, I was unable to walk and was tied into a wheelchair. Some doctors tried the tricks of the Shabak secret service on me. I once suffered badly on a rough ride in a prison vehicle to Ramle Jail where the place felt like a slaughterhouse.

Doctors appeared not to care, even when witnessing the emaciated bodies of myself and a fellow inmate, who had been on hunger strike for 200 days.

I was also placed in a room where there was the aroma of appetising food: roast beef, coffee and sweets.

I could hear myself saying, "Come on Ayman eat."

My body, willing to eat was talking to me. Dignity and I battled one another. Dignity won out and I denied food and refused to negotiate with the jailers.

The Occupiers conceded somewhat and decided that I should be expelled to Gaza. The Israelis are not trustworthy. I recall Samer El-Barq, who they promised to set free but reneged on the deal, as soon as he gave up his hunger strike.

I will only give up my hunger strike in Gaza I declared and was exiled there, where I ended my protest.

And where I first ate. ∎

Ayman Al-Sharawna is a 44-year-old former Palestinian political prisoner who is married with eleven children, the eldest of whom is 26 and the youngest is two. He spent thirteen years in Israeli jails and two years in the Palestinian Authority jails. He was released in October 2011 as part of the Shalit prisoners swap. He lives in the Gaza Strip having been deported from Hebron.

My Stomach Refused Force-feeding

Gerry Kelly
Ireland

I WAS a member of the Irish Republican Army when I was arrested in England in 1973 at the age of nineteen for bombing London. Along with a number of other comrades I was sentenced to two life terms, plus twenty years in prison.

We embarked on a hunger strike that same year on the basis of our demand to be transferred to a jail closer to our homes in the North of Ireland where IRA prisoners had political status.

I was in Wormwood Scrubs Prison in London.

On my nineteenth day, the Principal Medical Officer (PMO) came into my cell and said that if I didn't agree to take food voluntarily then he would force-feed me. When I refused, he informed me that he would be returning in half an hour to begin.

When they left, I used the time to barricade the cell door but to no avail as they brought in equipment to force the door open. I was sitting on the bed, naked except for a blanket wrapped around my waist, as I had refused to wear a criminal uniform.

The guards came flooding in and surrounded the bed. There were six or eight of them and they were getting in each other's way. They must have been expecting stronger resistance but they were dealing with someone who hadn't eaten food for nineteen days.

They had me subdued within a couple of minutes. At that stage I had lost around eighteen pounds in weight. I was about eleven stone when I first embarked on the strike. My spectacles had been the first casualty of the tussle and I had lost the blanket and my rosary beads in the struggle as well, so I was stark-naked. I was lying on my back pinned down by guards.

The doctor came into the cell and instructed the guards to pull me up the bed into a sitting position with my back against the tall metal bed-end. At that stage two guards were lying across my legs and two others had my arms pinned against the bed-end. Under the doctor's instruction, I was held tighter in the jack-knife position and my head was pulled back by the hair over the top bar of the bed-end.

"Open your mouth now!" Ordered the doctor.

I clenched my teeth, as I could not move my head to indicate my "No", and sensed that opening my mouth to answer was exactly what he needed.

"I've no time for this!" he said, impatiently.

One guard locked my head in a tight grip to prevent struggle and then someone leaned on my chin to try to open my mouth. Another tried forcing my nose upwards, causing it to bleed. Another stretched my lips apart in their attempt to force me to open my mouth. Knuckles were bored into my jaw-joints. Despite my weakened state, I realised that the jaw-muscles must be one of the strongest muscles in the body.

Eventually the doctor produced a Ryles Tube, which is a very narrow-gauge nasogastric feeding tube. It was made of hard plastic and he inserted it into my nose. As it hit the back of my throat I gagged. Immediately, one of the waiting guards shoved something between my teeth.

The object turned out to be a piece of wood containing a circular hole in its middle. The easiest way to describe it would be as a 'horse-bit'. I found out, moments later, that its purpose was to hold my teeth apart which would allow them to push much wider-gauge tubing down my throat.

I could see that the doctor had beckoned the female nurses in, who were pushing a metal trolley containing some equipment. The nurses looked shocked and it wasn't because I was naked. I, on the other hand, had become very aware of my nakedness but couldn't do anything about it.

The only part of my body that could move was my eyes, therefore I could not communicate my panic and fear as the rubber tube was pushed through the hole into my mouth. The tube made me dry-retch as it hit the flap at my throat. The epiglottis is a flap which is there to prevent food and drink being inhaled into the lungs. I was vividly aware that if the doctor had forced the tube down the wrong way, I would most likely die. I knew this because one of the governors had threatened me with the possibility. But I was also very aware that a previous IRA Volunteer, Thomas Ashe, had died this way while on hunger strike in Mountjoy Prison in Dublin, in 1917. In fact, force-feeding had never been used again in prisons in Ireland, after the huge public outrage at his death.

My feelings were of absolute helplessness and mental panic. The thick tube was lubricated with paraffin oil, but it was painful as it moved further inside me. At the end of the tube was a plastic funnel which was held above my face. My panic increased as I watched the doctor pour a thick, milk-coloured liquid into the funnel. This panic and absolute helplessness would recur every time I was force-fed and that was to take place one hundred and sixty-seven times – although I didn't know it at that moment.

When they were finished and the tube was removed, my stomach fought back as I heaved and vomited up most of the liquid which had been forced into me. My stomach had shrunk during the hunger strike and could not cope with that amount of food. The nurses never came to a force-feeding session again.

I was exhausted and emotional, but glad that I had resisted.

As the force-feeding continued, determination and levels of resistance would vary and fluctuate. There were some harder sessions to come and some easier, and my commitment was to be tested but never to breaking point. Now that I had experienced the process, waiting for the session to occur daily could, at times, be as bad as the action itself.

When I managed to prevent myself gagging, they changed to moving the hard tube back and forth in my nasal-passage knowing that it was rubbing against the sensitive mucous membrane. The effect was a sharp pain which felt like a knitting-needle was being pushed into the gap between the eyeball and the nose. That forced me to cry out and the wooden-bit was pushed in between my teeth. I fought against the pain. Sometimes I managed to prevent them from opening my mouth and they would leave – but always to return. Usually, a particularly brutal doctor would run large metal forceps up and down my gums until I couldn't bear the pain.

One of the less wholesome ideas that one doctor came up with, when I was throwing up, was to collect the vomit in a kidney dish and pour it back into my stomach. I found this, strangely, to be nearly as humiliating as having been naked in front of the nurses.

I was on hunger-strike for two hundred and five days before getting an agreement from the British Home Secretary that I and my three comrades, also on hunger strike and being force-fed, would indeed be transferred to Long Kesh Prison Camp outside Belfast, where many of our comrades were incarcerated. ■

Gerry Kelly, in his tenth year in jail, escaped from the H-Blocks of Long Kesh, when 37 prisoners shot their way to freedom. He was on the run for three years before being caught in Amsterdam, extradited to Ireland and returned to jail. After his release he was involved in secret contacts with the British government which paved the pave for the peace process. He was elected to the Stormont Assembly and served as a junior minister in government along with the late Martin McGuinness. He is the author of Words From A Cell (prison poems); The Escape; and a memoir, Playing My Part.

A Woman Alone

Hanna Shalabi
Palestine

I REMEMBER the night of 16 February, 2012, as cold dark skies chilled the winter air. Darkness prevailed and peace reigned, in the silent Barqin village which lies to the south west of Jenin city.

Suddenly a terrible sound caused panic, I recognised the noise of the stomping feet of Israeli soldiers with barking police dogs, on their way to surround our neighbourhood.

I wondered who the soldiers had come for, on that cold night. I was shocked as the Israeli troops barked, "Come out, come out," and called my sister, my mother, my brother Omar, his wife and my name.

They said they would only hold us for five minutes, then set us free.

My elderly father along with my oldest brother Amar stayed in our home with weapons pointed at their heads.

The soldiers turned everything upside down in our house as they searched closets, beds, clothes and in the process tore everything to pieces.

They prevented me from getting to the children to cuddle and calm either of them. Shlomo, an Israeli intelligence services officer shouted, "Hanna must die, arrest Hanna".

I could not believe it, but he was actually calling my name.

A male Israeli soldier grabbed me by the hand as another, a female searched me. "Stop," I screamed. "Do not touch me, I'm a Palestinian woman and you do not have the right to touch me."

I was stunned as a blow hit my face, and made me dizzy. "Oh God, what should I do? Who am I? Who are these people?" I thought.

I wondered where was humanity and dignity, when all they brought was darkness and pain.

Soldiers continued the terror as they beat me about my head with their guns.

They rained down blows on every inch of my body. "Oh mother, oh father, oh brothers," I cried as the soldiers hit every inch of my body from all sides.

As they hit my brother I called out, "Leave Omer alone, leave my brother alone, this is unjust."

I thought to myself, people all over the world were sleeping in peace and tranquillity, here we are in our homes, being hit by guns and sticks in the middle of the night.

Sholmo shouted, "You villain, get in the jeep," I froze, I didn't move. I said I would not take a step until I changed into my Islamic traditional clothes.

The soldier in charge refused my request and hit me again. "Get in the jeep," he ordered. I refused again.

Finally, they allowed me back into the house, accompanied by a female officer.

I took my clothes to another room when I heard soldiers shouting outside. Suddenly they burst in while I was naked. Although in pain, and unable to scream, I was moved to the army jeep.

Blindfolded, I was forced to squat in the back of a military jeep, everything was dark in the nightmare I was suffering.

Soldiers armed to the teeth accompanied us as we were driven to the Salem Military Centre near the city of Jenin.

I was sentenced to administrative detention without a charge against me.

I had to make a decision whether to die or live in dignity. I decided to go on hunger strike until I obtained my freedom from the clutches of the occupier.

As days went by, the hunger strike was taking its toll, my body was becoming weaker, I was having blackouts, my bones were protruding from my wasting body, my life was a misery.

On day forty-seven I declared that I would not abandon my strike, I would not be sentenced to administrative detention seven times without charge.

Oh, Allah, at last they have relented and I have achieved my liberty. Yes, sacrifice is the brother of freedom.

Now I will be expelled to Gaza, away from my family and friends, but moving to a part of my homeland and freedom means everything to me. ■

Hanna Shalabi is a 39-year-old former Palestinian political prisoner who was deported to Gaza where she got married after spending twenty seven months in Israeli jails. She was released in October 2011 as part of the Shalit swap deal, was re-arrested and then released in April 2012. She was deported to the Gaza Strip following a hunger strike she staged to protest her administrative detention. She lives in Gaza.

Light of Hope (1)

Dirar Al-Hroub
Palestine

FOR the thousandth time I said, "I don't know."
The Israeli interrogator torturing me didn't like my answer. I was held in a headlock while threatened at the same time, but I remained uncooperative.

I was holding back a volcano in my body and I then made up my mind not to give in to the oppressor.

Sitting behind his desk, drawing deeply on a cigarette and blowing out a cloud of smoke, the interrogator fixed his eyes on me and repeated his empty threats.

As a result of the torture, while being tied to a chair my exhausted body was experiencing excruciating pain and I'd lost the ability to lift my head.

This was to be expected on the fortieth day of a vicious investigation in the summer of 2012.

The Israeli intelligence officer was known for his use of extensive and cruel torture methods and his face reflected his evil nature.

After another round of interrogation, a volcano erupted in my mind, I stared into his narrow eyes in the middle of his hateful reddish face and declared, "From this moment on I am on hunger strike."

He laughed, believing I was responding to his threats, in a bid to stop the severe treatment he was handing out.

From then on, jailers and interrogators took more regular shifts to torture my body, which had lost all feelings.

Carrying out their evil plan, they would give me two-hour breaks between beatings to let blood flow back into my body, so I could suffer further pain from the severity of their torture.

A day later the door of my cell crashed open, a group of jailers surrounded me.

They forced me to stand, tied me up and blindfolded my eyes. I was taken to a tiny underground cell called 'exile' where there was no air, no light and no feeling of time, place or life. After a while, sitting in a corner I eventually managed to sleep.

They gave me food through a small hole in an iron door.

I felt that they were not taking my hunger strike seriously, but after three days they opened the door and found all the meals untouched.

Confused, they just stared at my weak body lying on the floor, unable to stand.

On the eighth day of the strike I was taken back to an interrogation session with a group of intelligence officers. They all attempted to persuade me to abandon my hunger strike because of the danger to my health, as if they were not killing me slowly every day.

Within forty-eight hours I lost consciousness. I later woke up tied to a bed, surrounded by white curtains and not knowing where I was.

A young girl peered through the curtains and looked shocked to see the shaking body of an emaciated man, covered with black, blue and red bruises.

She looked fearful and fled. I realised then that I was in a Jerusalem hospital.

A middle-aged nurse said, "I will let you go home if you wish".

At first, I didn't understand what she meant, but then realised she was trying to kill me.

She jerked a syringe from my arm, resulting in terrible pain, a torrent of blood flowed covering my bed, the curtains and floor.

A desperate bid to inject my neck was stopped by guards, who immediately took me back to prison.

I returned to Al-Muskoubiyya interrogation centre where I remained on hunger strike for twelve days until my fragile body forced them to submit to my demands. Paralyzed and on a stretcher, I was transferred to Ashkelon Prison. The prison chief approached me and said, "You should not think you won, you will be sentenced to life in prison, rot and die there.

"You will not get a pardon or be freed in a prisoner swap deal."

Lifting my heavy head, I said, "I promise, you will cry blood for every day you keep me here."

I felt the thud of his heavy hand on my face, concluding a dark chapter of my life in Al-Muskoubiyya.

After three years the prison chief carried out his threat of a sentence and I was given life in jail.

But the Palestinian resistance carried out its promise as well and I was liberated in the Promise of the Free Prisoner Swap deal.

Now here I am, telling the story for those who want to hear it, so that hope and justice will find its way through our sorrows and wounds. ■

Dirar Al-Hroub is a 55-year-old former Palestinian political prisoner who works as a journalist. He is a PhD Candidate in Educational Management. He was sentenced to life but was released ten years later as part of the Shalit prisoner swap deal in October 2011. He was deported from Ramallah and currently lives in the Gaza Strip.

© APA images

A demonstrator holding a bottle of water and salt.

Freedom Beckoned Me

Hassan Safadi
Palestine

ONCE on a summer's night the moon appeared sad, black clouds hung over my thoughts, I stared at the tangled stars as I tried to escape the thundering sounds of military vehicles. My breath was shackled as my dreams were held captive. Detention enraged me most of all.

The darkness of cells and chains of oppression engraved anger in my soul. A day seemed like a thousand days.

I had received four years of detention without being charged, I had to suffer administrative detention, which is nothing less than a life-taking rope around a prisoner's neck.

This time the occupier decided to sentence me to

severe administration as well. I raged and rejected this harsh punishment.

My blood boiled and my heart pumped wildly, in defiance of what could be a challenge to each living part of my body.

I sent letters to legal and humanitarian organisations. I told them about the injustice of my jailers. I had been sentenced to serve administrative detention over and over again.

I felt that the Israeli legal system and juries had danced all over my bleeding wounds. My legal and humanitarian pleas were in vain, no organisation replied, I remained locked behind bars in the treacherous occupier's cells, still searching for liberty.

I decided to fight for my freedom and the brightness of a life without terror or fear. The idea that I was sick and helpless forced me to battle on. "I will fight for my dignity," I declared.

I went on hunger strike, my will fed me and the thought of freedom obsessed me. A beacon of hope lit up my mind with the belief that the occupier would respond to my demands.

Days passed as if they were a whole eternity. I held tight to my right to freedom, even though part of me was deeply wounded.

At first I thought it would take days or weeks.

In my mind the arrogance of the occupation created a huge personal challenge. For me martyrdom was one choice, freedom the other.

Three months passed without food or drink. My refusal to take food, I humbly offered up to Allah, and my drink was only water with salt. I kept praying to Allah.

The looks on the faces of the Zionist officers who wanted me dead, will never leave me, but I stared right back at them.

I was imprisoned, but free. They were the tyrants.

The days were long, I tasted both physical and psychological bitterness. I vomited blood, I could not move or walk.

My senses became weaker. Worst of all they took me to Ramle cemetery to frighten and humiliate me.

One day I erupted in response to the insults of my jailers, I spat out strong words and was pushed from my wheelchair to the ground as pain spread all over my dying body. I could not retreat; I was in the middle of an irreversible process. I had to choose between freedom or martyrdom.

The Shabak, the secret service agents of the Israelis, got my message and tried to kill me several times by further sentencing me to administrative detention.

My soul was determined to come out victorious, in spite of the pains which invaded every part of my body. They sometimes humiliated me by locking me up with common Israeli criminals. I was thrown into solitary confinement many other times, where I couldn't recognise night from day.

When death threatened to take me, my soul and body were ready but dawn broke on the horizon for me.

I was laid on a bed, in an unused hospital, that had no medical care.

A lawyer informed me that after a hundred and sixty-six days of hunger strike, the jailers had capitulated to my demands.

I would go free. I thanked Allah.

The walls of the prison are witness to how I smashed the arrogance of the occupier and obtained my liberty. ∎

Hassan Safadi is a 41-year-old former Palestinian political prisoner who is married and was administratively arrested many times for a total of more than eleven years. He was released in December 2017 and lives in Nablus in the West Bank.

When My Blood Lights Up

Khader Adnan
Palestine

I TOOK a few steps from my home and into the warmth of the sun. Green lands perfumed with the scent of Palestine carried me.

Good and bad memories came to mind, I had always longed to see this lush pastured scene.

But now in my thoughts I was surrounded by cold walls that blocked light, air and the far-off horizon.

Detention works side-by-side with oppression and death.

I had spent five years in jail on two occasions. The allegations on my indictments were mainly my national loyalty.

I once received a written order from the Israeli intelligence service to sit for an investigation. I tore it to pieces because I didn't want my life to be underestimated. At that time, I started to incite young people to resist detention and oppose investigations into their lives.

Our freedom is the most precious thing we have.

Prison cells have always worsened our wounds and increased our suffering.

I convinced others, mainly the youth to resist unfair detention, even though it would result in them being wanted by the Israeli police and force them to disappear and hide away.

This action works against the occupier and instils the spirit of challenge within the hearts of young Palestinians.

A few months later I was detained again – for the ninth time.

Being locked in a dark dungeon, where Israeli soldiers beat my chained body was deeply humiliating and oppressing.

Their punches and their weapons have left permanent scars on my body. Their barbarism itself stood before me, literally.

For them, I was just a number. The jailers tried to rip away my dignity but I treasured my freedom and held tight to patience.

Freedom beckoned me from the moment I was first imprisoned, it haunted me. My quest for liberty also drove me to bolster the morale of my friends and brothers.

I came to the idea of how I could break the chains and destroy the arrogance of the jailer by declaring that I would go on hunger strike, alone.

I knew what the consequences might be, but freedom is precious and martyrdom is honourable.

I went on hunger strike, I counted on nothing except belief in my Lord.

Time for me was unlimited, every day passed like a year, each day became heavier than the day before. Mentally it wasn't easy at all. However, I was determined to teach the occupiers a lesson in dignity and defiance. They, the occupiers, spared no means in their bid to weaken me.

I will never forgive their insults; I was usually showered by the jailers. I will not forget how they moved my weak, faint and emaciated body from one prison to another, even my organs collapsed.

They tried to kill me by neglecting me medically. I cannot forget what they did, even now. They tried to weaken me.

Their hatred, oppression and brutality still live with me.

They pretend to act humanely it front of the rest of the world, but they don't. Once they forced me into court when I couldn't walk, I was surrounded by dozens of soldiers and judges. In my mind the judges acted, not like real judges, they inflamed the spirit of defiance in me.

I screamed, "The hunger strike continues until I get my freedom, dignity and honour." The courtroom shook.

The words I had spoken brought me from weakness to strength, from exhaustion to wellbeing.

They quickly got me out of the court. They wanted to extinguish my voice.

For sixty-six days, I refused food, I did not eat and just drank salt with water. I called it the Sol of Dignity.

During my struggle I occupied my mind by recalling the sun on the distant green lands. I missed most of all the feel of grains of sand, the scent of the almond and lemon trees.

My resistance proved that the occupier will never understand our story and our love for our land.

My health deteriorated completely. They harassed and pressured me.

They wanted me to end my hunger strike and negotiate, I bluntly refused. Determination made me stronger, I demanded to go home, to my family, to my daughters, who had spent long periods of their childhoods without me since I was jailed.

In the end the occupier gave in to my demands and I was to be freed after a short time.

I thanked Allah, I prostrated myself, I ended my hunger strike.

Knowing that I was not the only one who had to resort to a hunger strike, my soul always smiles when my fellow prisoners rebel against the occupier.

Free we are, free we were born. ■

Khader Adnan is a 43-year-old former Palestinian political prisoner who works now as a baker and is married with eight children. He spent eight years in Israeli jails in separate terms and was released in November 2018. He currently lives in Jenin in the West Bank.

*Two female protesters distribute a cup of water and salt to introduce
Palestinians to the experience of hunger strike.*

© APA images

In the Presence of Brothers

Khalil Abu Aram

I am in the presence of brothers,
in a meadow of camomile.

Its breeze scented by liquorice and poppy,
bedewed with wildflowers.

Its crystals are grape and lemon
and a carpet swathed in purple.

Its stars are orange and pomegranate,
a reflection tinged with amber.

Its fragrance is wild thyme – rich is its soil.
Its coffee, aromatic with saffron and affection.

I am in the presence of saints,
in the garden of childhood, in all its innocence.

Its watchman is a demon.

I am at the convergence of worldly and spiritual blessing,
and the torment of regulation.

I am in a paradise fabricated by man.
Our Eden is enclosed with gunfire.

So Much Went Unspoken

Laurence McKeown
Ireland

FOUR comrades had already died on hunger strike before I joined the fast on 29 June, 1981. Well before then I had received a 'comm' from the IRA's Army Council. It read simply, "Comrade, you have put your name forward for the hunger strike. Do you know that this means you will most likely be dead within two months? That means, comrade, that you will be no more. Reconsider carefully your decision. AC."

Those may not be the exact words but the communication was as blunt as that. I hadn't expected it and the words did startle me at first. Seeing my 'death' written in black and white appeared very stark but it didn't cause me to rethink my position. I was ready to go ahead.

When I began the hunger strike, I weighed ten and a half stone (66.6 kg), about two stone underweight for my height. My heart, lungs, and blood pressure were checked by the prison doctor and I was generally in good shape. I had never been in hospital or suffered any serious illness in the past so I wasn't too concerned in that regard. I was asked to read and sign a form which stated I was aware of what I was doing and that doctors would not intervene medically unless I so requested.

Coldness was what I felt first; my feet especially. The heating in the Block was off for the summer and when I complained about this, I was told the boiler was being renewed. I got extra blankets. At one time I had seven of them covering me and some of those were folded over, making it about ten or eleven layers of clothing over me. Only then did I feel warm enough. No doubt drinking the cold water didn't help, though I noticed that when I was moved to the prison hospital (after twenty-one days on hunger strike), which also had no heat on, I didn't feel the same degree of coldness. In fact, I slept with just the usual issue of bedclothes covering me. Possibly, I was becoming accustomed to it, though my feet still felt cold.

If you go for a considerable number of hours without food, or if you expect a meal then don't get it, you begin to think of food and what you are missing. A hunger strike is different. I knew I wasn't going to eat. It wasn't that I was denied food or missed a meal. I had decided I wasn't going to eat and I knew the reasons why. The sense of hunger that would exist on other occasions didn't therefore arise. Of course, there was a feeling of emptiness but not hunger pangs.

Meals were, however, placed on the table in my cell every day; breakfast remained there until lunchtime when it was removed and replaced with lunch. That meal then sat there until the evening when it was removed in place of supper. The food on my table had no appeal to me and it wouldn't have mattered how delicious it was.

I received many letters and cards during the hunger strike and was grateful for every one of them. I knew people found it difficult knowing what to say in them, or whether or not, for instance, they should refer to the brilliant holiday they were having. The most they could do was wish me all the best and say how they were thinking and praying for me. It didn't really matter though what they wrote, it was just nice to receive the correspondence. I got a few from people I hadn't heard from since coming into jail, and one from a woman who had written several letters to me during the Blanket protest but which I had never received. It brought back many happy memories and made me laugh in some places but I didn't write much myself and even then, only in the early stages of the fast. As time went on, I couldn't motivate myself to put pen to paper.

Time dragged by fairly slowly in the prison hospital but the nights were the longest, though I looked forward to 'lock up' at 8.30pm, just to be on my own. While my sight was still good, I read the newspapers and did the odd crossword. Apart from writing the occasional letter I listened to the radio most of the time, though it was more a case of the radio providing background music than me actually listening to it. As time went on, I listened to the radio less and less, though strangely during this time my taste in music changed. Normally, I could enjoy most types of music with the exception of Irish Country & Western. I loathe it. Yet during the latter part of the fast it was the only music I could listen to. The only explanation I can offer is that it is so boring and repetitive that it requires no thought – you can just switch it on and let it drone away.

I thought of my family often and of how the hunger strike was affecting them. I knew my mother was the one bearing the brunt of the pressure. She was the one most in contact with me, she was the one who had visited me most regularly since my imprisonment, and she was the one who felt most deeply for me. She was not a republican and I wondered how she felt being to the fore in this form of republican struggle. I knew that her thoughts would be with everyone on the hunger strike and especially with their families. I regretted I hadn't more time and better circumstances to speak with her on the visits but also realised that I was often avoiding talk of what she meant to me as it would be just too emotional for both of us. So instead, I presented the jovial face when we met on visits and spoke of how well I felt.

In my mind I relived many exploits with old friends. In fact, because the years spent on the blanket protest involved recounting old stories of our youth, the images were familiar to me. I had nothing in common with most of these people by this time, having drifted apart over the years, but their earlier friendship was still dear to me. You might say that after 8.30 at night I wasn't really in the hospital but off in either bygone days or living in a future H-Block with political status and all the freedom of movement and pastime that permitted.

Like the prison camp in general, the hospital ward is very, very quiet at night, and although I know it sounds like a cliché, I was often simply listening to the silence. At such times I felt very close to the ones in the Blocks. I knew they would be thinking of us, asking for news about us, writing to whoever they could on our behalf, and in some cases preparing to join the hunger strike themselves. The nights were long but I enjoyed the solitude.

The weakness that gradually took over in my body seemed to be paralleled in my mind. After fifty days or so I found difficulty in maintaining interest in conversation. I wasn't the only one who appeared to feel this way, and all dialogue between us (on hunger strike) was of short comments interspersed with long periods of silence. It wasn't melancholy or depressed; it was simply tiredness and a disinterest in most topics which we, or anyone, would normally be concerned about. I found that increasingly I had little in common with those I met other than the other hunger strikers. Others lived a different life from me. Or maybe it was that they simply lived a life, whereas I knew that mine would soon end. The things they seemed anxious about seemed ludicrous to me. It was difficult therefore to express any real interest in what was taking place around me. In the last days of my fast this was also the case with the protest and hunger strike itself. I certainly wanted to see it succeed but by this stage had accepted that I wouldn't live to see that. My focus was on living out my last days as comfortably as possible. Death now began to appear more as a release from my weak and troublesome body.

I noticed that when a hunger striker was about two, certainly no more than three, days away from death their bowels would open. I believe I first identified it in the case of Tom McElwee. It was followed by a marked deterioration in Tom's condition. The bowel movement itself wasn't the cause of deterioration but it was an indication that the person was in the very last stages of life. One night Micky Devine (one of the hunger strikers, and the last of the ten men to die) told me in the canteen where we were out for 'association time' that he had had diarrhoea most of that day. I already knew, as one of the Medical Officers had told me. I said nothing other than to ask if he was OK, and he said he was. Both of us knew what it signalled. Micky was already very weak by this stage, though because his features were less sharp, he didn't appear as gaunt as others, such as Kieran Doherty, Kevin Lynch, and Tom McElwee. This was the last night we talked together. The following day he didn't get out of bed and his family were allowed to stay in the hospital until his passing. I could hear them going in and out of his cell for the few days that he lingered on but didn't go in myself as I would've felt I was intruding. Amongst the hunger strikers there were no goodbyes said, only, "See you". His death occurred silently. All that was heard was the dull 'thud' the light metal trolley made as it knocked against the wall, manoeuvring through the doorway of his cell, weighted by his lifeless body.

By this time, I was very weak though I was still getting up for a while each day. I was less interested in what was happening around me and I knew I was preparing myself for death as I had joined the hunger strike a week behind Micky and was now the longest on it. As I grew progressively weaker and realised the imminence of my death, my thoughts were mostly about the manner in which I would die. I had already witnessed others dying and in different ways. I hoped it would be sudden like Big Tom McElwee and without sickness.

I thought about Tom's death a lot, probably because it was the most vivid to me, having spoken together the previous night and having seen him that morning. He had been relatively free from sickness throughout the fast and my own health and rate of deterioration up until then had very much mirrored this. I therefore looked on Tom's death as the most likely example of how I would die. That is, I would be lucid right up to the very end then suffer a coronary attack or some other instantaneous form of death. That wasn't a morbid thought at the time. It was relevant to my circumstances. I had witnessed other men suffering the pain of sickness and had listened to the torments of Paddy Quinn and knew that Martin Hurson had endured the same pain before finally dying. So, the manner in which Tom died was therefore very much to be desired.

The actual fact of dying, of being no more, didn't occupy my mind a lot. Possibly there was a reluctance to dwell on that as it as it would have seemed to rule out the possibility of victory. I would always think positively, as I am inclined to by nature. I would also, for as long as it was possible, get up each day and walk about for a while or even just sit on the armchair beside my bed. I was assisted and encouraged in this by Paul Lennon, one of the Prison Medical Officers, who made sure we didn't allow ourselves to become dejected.

In the last days of my fast, death took on a more real appearance and was now an inevitability rather than a possibility. But by then I was totally exhausted and to even think such things in any deep sense, or for any length of time, takes a lot of concentration so I didn't dwell on it. Only in those last few days did they stop leaving food in my cell. I had complained to them before about the smell of it once it cooled but they said they were legally obliged to provide me with food. At this stage, though, they conceded that I probably couldn't eat that type of food even if I did decide to eat. The cell door was also locked during the night and Paul Lennon protested about this. He said it was illogical, as well as being dangerous. They agreed to leave it open. I had been on hunger strike for about sixty-five days at this stage and they had begun to give me a body rub every few hours to improve circulation and stop sores from forming on the skin of my back and hips where my body's weight was pressing down. I was also given a sheepskin rug to lie on, which greatly helped.

Someone came in to visit me one day and I still don't know if he was a doctor or an official from the Northern Ireland Office. He was with a few others, besides the prison doctor, and he strutted around my bed asking a few questions about how I felt. Initially, I replied to his questions but as his manner was noticeably abrupt, I began to look away and ignore him. He stopped at the end of my bed and in a loud clear voice told me what was happening to my body.

"These purple marks on your chest and arms are blood vessels which have broken down and collapsed. Your eyesight has been permanently damaged. Your vital organs are under intense strain at this moment. There are a number of ways you will possibly die: a brain tumour or a massive coronary attack. Your kidneys or liver could collapse at any moment. Either way you can expect to die very shortly."

He turned on his heel and walked out the door, apparently more upset at my impending death than I was.

I was more concerned with the practicalities of dying than with the actual event. I was becoming increasingly sick, the first time during the hunger strike that I had experienced sickness. I don't know if it was because my intake of water had reduced, because I found it increasingly difficult to drink it, but I made a determined effort to increase my water consumption and the sickness got no worse. What did worsen was the onset of hiccups which came after about sixty-seven days. They remained with me almost constantly and just as a bout of them would stop and I was getting relief, I would move in the bed and they would begin all over again. I couldn't hear so clearly and was having headaches at times. Bright lights really annoyed me so the cell light was left off.

When I had a bowel movement, I knew I had not long left to live. It was on a Friday afternoon and the sensation was no different from feeling the need to go to the toilet in normal circumstances. However, it became quite painful given that in my case it had been more than eight weeks since I last had a bowel movement. The Medical Officers gave me suppositories, which helped, I suppose. Nevertheless, I still spent about an hour in the toilet and was exhausted when I was finished. I was already in a very weak condition but this spent my last reserves of strength. Bobby Hagan, one of the prison orderlies who was always very kind to all of us on hunger strike, assisted me back down to my cell and into bed. I didn't get out of it again. I knew that I now had no more than two to three days left to live, if that, but I was too tired to dwell on that thought. In fact, in many ways it appeared inviting; more or less a release.

Some hunger strikers' families had been with them for a long period of time before their deaths. They would sleep in an empty cell in the prison ward and one of them would always be with the man on hunger strike. In Kieran Doherty's case his family had come in when he was fifty days on hunger strike because he had taken very ill at that time. However, he picked up again and lived for almost another three weeks, during which time his family were always with him. After this, families were not allowed in until it was very apparent the hunger striker was going to die or, as in the case of Big Tom, they did not get entry at all because he died suddenly. A Doctor Bell came to see me when I was sixty-eight days on hunger strike and after he asked me a few questions about how I felt, Paul Lennon, who had accompanied him, strongly recommended that my family be allowed in. Paul said that medically it could not be said that I was on the point of death but everyone knew that I could die at any minute given the length of time I had been on hunger strike and the experience of those who had already died. Dr Bell seemed to consider it for a few moments then nodded his head that he would give permission for my family to come into the hospital. They came that night.

My recollection of this period of the hunger strike is not so clear in terms of the order in which events occurred. I remember my sister Mary coming in with my mother. Mary was in a distressed state and asked me if I intended continuing with the fast. I said I did and she began sobbing loudly. My mother sat beside her looking over to me, expressionless. I knew that out of all of them she would be the one who was most calm, while bearing not only the burden of her own sorrow but the weight of comforting others. I talked about some neighbours and friends and generally tried to make some conversation to show that I was lucid and in good spirits. I knew it distressed them when I was sick, particularly when they saw how much the hiccups drained me. My dad came in to see me but just stood in the corner of the cell for a while and went out again. He was unable to speak. Eugene, my brother, also visited and appeared to be handling it OK. On the Saturday I was dozing, in and out of sleep or consciousness. I kept dreaming that I was in some place totally surrounded by blackness and that I felt very, very tired and wanted to sleep but kept saying to myself, "You mustn't sleep, you mustn't sleep or you're a goner." It seemed like the last fight of the ego to hold onto life.

Members of my family kept a constant vigil at my bedside. When I would wake, they would ask me if I was OK and pass me a drink of water if I asked. I don't know when exactly I began to lose consciousness but the last time I recall coherently talking to anyone was on the Saturday evening. My mother had been at my bedside on her own. She had never said to me at any time since joining the hunger strike, or even when I had first told her that I could possibly be on it, not to do so. She had never discouraged me in any way but had worked in every way possible with anyone who wanted to help our protest. We had never discussed the likely consequences of my going on hunger strike, both knowing what could happen, and we left it at that. So much went unspoken between us. I knew that when she was out of my cell, she was across the ward on her knees praying and when she would return to me, she would still have that calm face even though she was feeling her sorrow intensely. That evening I said to her, "I'm sorry that all this had to come about for you." She leaned across to me and whispered, "You know what you have to do and I know what I have to do."

I lost consciousness after that. It was the sixty-ninth day of my fast. The following day, in the afternoon, my mother authorised medical intervention. I regained consciousness in the Intensive Care Unit of the Royal Victoria Hospital in Belfast. ■

Dr Laurence McKeown is an author, playwright, and filmmaker. He served 16 years in the H-Blocks of Long Kesh Prison, 1976 – 1992. He was co-editor of the book, Nor Meekly Serve My Time, *which was updated and reissued in 2021 by Beyond The Pale.*

A Ray of Light

Mohammed Al-Qeeq
Palestine

DURING my hunger strike an inner voice drew me into a dream that I experienced in minute detail. Gone were the pains of an aching body and missing too was the deafening silence in the darkness, now there was only a clear ray of light in the distance.

In my dream, my child's smile appeared in the middle of nowhere, as if God was telling me she was struggling to say my name, struggling with endless words of sorrow. I must tell you my little daughter, that I opened my arms wide to embrace you in your innocence and your scent penetrated my mind, your sparkling smiles, my little one, brought joy to my dream.

I was awoken by the horrors of my jailer screaming and ordering us to stand, so he could count our shadows.

I can now testify, how I was barely able to stand, as an eighteen-year-old hiding behind his military uniform and gun, attempted to count me and my fellow prisoners. Looking at my feet, I thanked God that I was still able to stand.

My memory also took me back to February 2016 and the Israeli hospital of Affula.

Lying like a dead man, I could only move my eyes which took their strength from God, my body was broken and ready for death. I was entering my third month of a hunger strike and was protesting over the injustice of being placed under administrative detention.

I was not thinking about my wife and family, who were waiting and hoping for good news that could keep me alive.

Hope kept them from fearing that one day I would just be a sad memory. I was only thinking about my creator, the Almighty. I cursed those who oppressed me and insisted that I should suffer oppression and injustice in a bid to make me give up my protest.

It was not just about my freedom, but rather the freedom of every soul who curses the injustice, just as I do. I was lying on my bed, caught between the manic screeching of soldiers and in my mind the prayers of campaigners who supported our just cause.

I could not keep up with their prayers nor was I able to recite them, but God knows I was able to keep them in my heart.

My screams filled the room as I was experiencing muscle spasms. I did not care at first but the pain made me cry out uncontrollably. I tried to hold the parts of my body that ached but eventually I passed into unconsciousness.

I was awoken to the joy of the news that I could end my hunger strike, after the occupation forces agreed to my right to freedom.

In a weak and exhausted voice, I thanked God for my victory. For me freedom felt like the sweetest scent of perfume. It was my elixir of life. I learned what freedom is by being hungry. But God's will be different, I would return to prison after only eight months of freedom.

A judge, who had no case against me, placed me under administrative detention once again.

After I was placed in a grave-like cell I immediately declared, "I will not take food". Thirty-three days of the strike had passed and my emaciated body was affected by illness and multiple health complications.

I had barely recovered from the suffering of my previous protest by refusing to take food. Now in less than a year I was back on hunger strike.

I ended my administrative detention again and put a final date to it, contrary to the previous times in which the occupation's intelligence used to do so.

Now, once again in a dream, the laughter of my little girl penetrated the prison walls and I am holding my beautiful daughter in my arms as she cries out in joy.

I am still in prison, I crave to live in the free world, I serve a sentence, a burden that was placed on me without committing a crime. This sentence highlights the oppression by holding me without a charge.

Yet, for every free person who has wrongly suffered under the occupier's hatred and injustices, a hunger striker feeds his personal dignity and fulfils his commitment in the quest for human rights. ∎

Palestinian journalists express solidarity with their colleague Mohammed Al-Qeeq who was on hunger strike in an Israeli jail.

Mohammed Al-Qeeq is a 38-year-old former Palestinian political prisoner who is married with three children. He works as a journalist. He was arrested five times and spent four years in prison. He was on hunger strike for six months. He was released in May 2016 while he was on hunger strike. He lives in Ramallah in the West Bank.

The Path to Revolution

Ali Asafra
Palestine

IN the cell I ran my fingers over my head which was starting to feel numb. For some strange reason I laughed and my fellow hunger strikers around me began to laugh too. It was an unusual time for such cheerfulness, but as they say: if you can find a reason to cry; there are a hundred reasons to laugh.

My weak, emaciated body with protruding bones and tightened skin told the story of my hunger strike. Our aim was to reclaim dignity by battling the injustices which we were subjected to in the prison cells.

I forced myself to have no interaction with my body, so that I would have no justification to surrender to my jailers.

We sat in the cells of Ishel prison, refusing to eat food or drink water in conditions unfit for human beings.

We desperately wanted to serve our unjust sentences and the loss of our liberty with the dignity all mankind deserve.

Some days later a rich aroma of food filled our cell, it was especially strange to us, as our empty stomachs had not had any nourishment for weeks.

It wasn't long before we recognised the flavoured smell of meat being barbecued in the prison.

This was a desperate bid by the Israeli Prison Service, along with a group of common criminals in an adjacent section of the jail, to try and force us to break our strike. They tried with no success, to tempt us with all kinds of meats being cooked at their 'barbecue party'.

Even to this day, I feel so proud at our steadfast refusal to break our strike, the same pride I still feel each time I retell this story to people I meet for the first time.

One action I will always remember is how three young hunger strikers faced an ordeal that was planned for them.

They had been transferred to a different cell, on the pretext of attending a court appearance session.

In their new cell, they slept on the floor and were awoken to find a table, laden with all kinds of foods and fruits.

Each of the men adamantly refused to fall for the cruel trick of offering them quality nourishment.

The men were then punished and beaten for refusing to break their strike.

During the last few days of the strike, which went on for twenty days, the prison administration distributed pamphlets warning about the health implications of not taking food.

One of our fellow inmates stood up and said, "They mentioned that we might lose our hair." We stared at his face for a short while and then burst out laughing. Minutes later he returned from the washroom with his head shaved. "If the problem is losing hair, I have no hair to lose," he said.

Our thirsty, hungry bodies rocked with laughter. Afterwards a group of us shaved our heads to express our indifference to everything the jailers were trying to do to us. The sound of our laughter brought the prison director rushing to us and I'll never forget the look of confusion on his face.

He was shocked and angry and started screaming. He asked me why I shaved my head, "My hair bothers me," I said.

While his big eyebrows bristled wet with sweat droppings, his face turned red with fury.

He accused me of lying. I answered him again, "We removed the hair you feared would be lost and will continue our hunger strike," I vowed. ■

Ali Asafra is a 39-year-old former Palestinian political prisoner and poet who spent nine years in Israeli jails. He is originally from the West Bank village of Biet Kahil and he was deported to the Gaza Strip upon his release as part of the Shalit prisoner swap deal in 2011.

Light of Hope (2)

Dirar Al-Hroub
Palestine

A WONDERFUL dream leads me on a stroll to an exotic land where I was enchanted by everything around me.

I didn't ask myself how I got there after I climbed to the top of a mountain. Outstretched below me lay a lush green plain with a river that looked like it was made of glass.

A girl stood on the far side of the river bank and waved to me. I didn't recognise her but she was extremely beautiful.

She called, "Why don't you come over to me?"

I attempted to cross the river but failed. Looking back, the magnificent landscape began to fade just like a mirage. I rubbed my eyes to focus but the mystical scene disappeared.

With my fantasy over I awoke on a rusty bed in a dingy, grey-walled cell and felt suffocated by my stinking brown clothes.

Glancing around, I realised I'd gone from my heavenly dream to a grey cell that felt like hell.

The walls seemed to be closing in on us as we struggled to take deep breaths, just to get some of the small amount of fresh air available.

Some of my fellow inmates scattered around the cell had beautiful dreams like mine, and they feared the shock of waking up from their fantasies to the reality of their prison hell.

We were some of the dozens of hunger strikers trying to win our basic human rights in Nafha Prison in 2004.

At visiting time, barriers deprived us of seeing our visitors clearly. The screens prevented us from looking into the eyes of the ones we loved.

It was painful for us to witness how our mothers were broken-hearted, knowing their sons were only given rotten food and confined to small dark cells, without sunlight and fresh air.

To end these and other injustices imposed on us by the prison authorities we went on hunger strike.

On the fourteenth day of the strike I woke up, stood and prepared to wash and pray. I began to wipe water off my hands and realised I had lost the ability to feel any strength in my legs.

I couldn't stand anymore, my body collapsed on the floor and I went into a state of unconsciousness.

My previous dream came back to me and I felt the girl beckoning me from the bank on the other side of the mystic river may have meant my final departure.

After a while I could sense some shadows and heard my name whispered repeatedly. I opened my eyes and found myself surrounded by fellow inmates who were trying to wake me from my short, hunger-induced coma. I assured them that I was fine and tried to find my balance and stand again.

I could not feel my feet, I couldn't get up, I heard someone say, "Maybe he's paralyzed." I tried in vain to rise again, but was too weak.

In our protest we had decided to boycott the prison clinic as a means of putting pressure on the prison service during the strike.

Of course, I refused to go to the clinic despite my deteriorating health. The prison director threatened that if I didn't go to the clinic, I would receive a brutal punishment.

I didn't care and remained determined to continue my hunger strike.

An hour later we heard the marching of soldiers' feet. We suspected that they were about to storm our section.

We were right, they burst in, took nine prisoners and left me on my own. I was dragged to the centre of the cell by a number of the soldiers and brutally beaten. They then searched all our belongings; I thought their mission was over but it hadn't even started.

Almost every part of me screamed in pain as they beat my fragile body black and blue with sticks and left marks on every inch of me.

For more than thirty minutes, twelve soldiers took turns at punching my emaciated body. I thought I would die after one of their blows to my chest nearly asphyxiated me.

They left my body, now just a pile of bones and flesh on the cell floor, trying to breath. I was like helpless prey mauled by dogs.

In a moment of calm, I sat in the centre of the cell feeling their hatred but I wore a smile and despite being breathless I whispered to myself, "Alright, the pain will go away tomorrow, but the hunger strike will continue." ■

Dirar Al-Hroub is a 55-year-old former Palestinian political prisoner who works as a journalist. He is a PhD Candidate in Educational Management. He was sentenced to life but was released ten years later as part of the Shalit prisoner swap deal in October 2011. He was deported from Ramallah and currently lives in the Gaza Strip.

God Saved Me from Death

Rawda Habib
Palestine

PERHAPS the most difficult decision faced by a prisoner is to engage in a hunger strike in a bid to gain his or her rights from the Israeli Prison Service (IPS), where a prisoner faces their jailers on an empty stomach.

I am freed prisoner Rawda Habib from the Al-Shujaea neighbourhood in Gaza.

In 2007, I was twenty-nine, married with four children but my life changed when I was arrested and sentenced to eight years in prison.

After my arrest and the interrogation ended, I was immediately placed in solitary confinement.

I asked to be moved to the female prisoners' room. The IPS didn't respond to my request, so I decided to go on open-ended hunger strike.

I didn't really know what going on a hunger strike meant. This was my first experience of it and I had only heard about the protests from news reports.

The jailers brought me my first meal after I was placed in solitary confinement. I handled it back as with the second and third.

I told the jailer that I was on hunger strike until the IPS responded to my request to be moved to the female prisoners' section.

Unlike other strikers who usually just refuse food, I resolved to stop eating and drinking water.

I was on the verge of death, a severe headache made me feel I was losing my mind and I thought I would go mad.

Everything seemed to be spinning, I felt so dizzy. I had severe pains in my stomach, kidneys and legs and I couldn't stand.

Hunger played tricks with my mind and I could see many different colours and felt strange sensations.

I didn't know that usually a hunger striker stops eating food and only takes salt with water, so as their stomachs don't rot. I also discovered that a striker could just about tolerate the hunger but not thirst. Not taking water can lead to paralysis, renal failure or even death within a few days.

On the evening of the third day I collapsed and fell to the ground. The jailers took me directly to the female prisoners' section to prevent me from dying.

When I arrived, my face was a pale yellow as if no blood was running through my veins, it was as if I was on a journey to death.

I ended my strike and remained in the prisoners' rooms until my release. While there I discovered more about the plight of hunger strikers in the prison.

Jailers would often provoke inmates on hunger strike by offering them cooked food. They would often barbecue food in the kitchens or at the jail gates and let the aroma of grilled meat drift through the strikers' rooms.

Jail authorities would also improve the quality of the food fed to other inmates, so as to entice strikers away from their protest.

Attempts to halt the protests by the authorities were all in vain as hunger strikers would never give up until their demands were met.

In many cases only God could help prisoners who fought their battles unseen by human rights organisations, because Israeli occupation forces hide cases of torture, beatings and humiliation along with the denial of human rights in their prisons.

In 2009, as part of a prisoner exchange deal, a Palestinian resistance group handed over a sixty second tape of the Israeli soldier, Gilad Shalit, proving to the Israeli occupation that he was alive. The exchange led to the release of female Palestinian prisoners from Israeli jails including myself. ■

Rawda Habib is a former Palestinian political prisoner who spent two years and a half in Israeli jails where she gave birth. She was released on in October 2009 as part of the first stage of the Shalit prisoner swap deal, during which a dozen female prisoners were released in exchange for a video showing Shalit alive. She lives in the Gaza Strip.

© Issam Rimawi

A Palestinian protester holds a banner that calls for ending administrative detention which allows Israel to detain Palestinians without charge or trial based on secret evidence.

Nothing Separates Paradise and Hellfire

Khalil Abu Aram

Nothing separates paradise and hellfire
except a straight path:
an unbroken line.
Whoever crosses it intact is saved
and wins wide-hipped, heavenly maidens.
But whoever swerves from truth into misguidance,
how can he carry on?
For the revolution is hell for the occupier.
A blazing light for every ally and every volunteer.
Liberation is the end:
no limit, no breach.
So you, who has made the free choice of resistance,
take back what belongs to the revolution,
then carry on.
The union of character and conviction
is easily made,
for the one who hopes for it,
a possession already gained.
The Revolution will stand firm against the enemy;
the one who wavers has gone astray.

But Revolutionaries will forever remain a badge of honour
for their people,
always on guard for the enemy.
No one is a loser in revolution
except the cowardly, the impatient,
or the one who does not dare.
Strive for the cause of struggle and freedom,
without fear, like a lioness unleashed.
You will win one of two heavens:
Victorious or viceroy to victory.
Join your past to present
and you will cease to be mortal.
Your future will be here.

The Feelings Are Still Raw

Mary Doyle
Ireland

I WAS born in Greencastle, on the outskirts of North Belfast, not far from Bobby Sands, whom I knew well. We in the Catholic community suffered discrimination and sectarian abuse. I knew it was related to our history and the fact that Britain had divided my country. I decided to join Cumann na mBann (a militant women's organisation connected to the IRA).

As a result of my activism I was arrested and charged with the attempted murder of two RUC (police) men but was actually convicted and sentenced to jail for five years for causing an explosion. At this time, we in Armagh Prison had political status.

At that time there were over one hundred of us and there was strength in numbers. For example, when the men burned down Long Kesh camp in 1974 we in Armagh took the governor hostage and barricaded the landing until we received reassurances that our comrades were safe.

I was in prison when loyalists bombed Conways Bar, where my parents were customers. My mother, Marie, was killed in the explosion. She was thirty-eight. A year earlier two Catholics civilians had also been killed in Conways in a sectarian loyalist attack.

I reported back to the IRA after my release but was caught within twelve months, along with two others, in September 1977. At my trial I refused to recognise the court and was sentenced to eight years for possession of incendiary devices.

The governors and screws took great satisfaction in telling me I was now 'a criminal'. I joined my comrades, eventually numbering twenty, on the protest. Unlike the men in the H-Blocks we were allowed to wear our own clothes but for refusing to do menial prison work and take orders we were confined to our cells and restricted to one visit a month. We lost parcels, letters and remission and our full entitlement to association. My father was in ill-health and it was my two brothers and my aunt who visited and looked after my needs as best they could.

The screws were abusive, particularly during cell searches. They seized all clothing coloured black – even though the clothes had come in through the censor – because we would wear black tops and skirts to commemorate our patriot dead on occasions such as Easter Sunday.

Prison officers were responsible for an escalation in the protest. They refused to let us out of our cells to empty the chamber pots. There were two prisoners to a cell and the pots were overflowing. When they opened the doors, we slopped it out onto the landing. They moved us to another wing and locked us up there. That's when the no wash protest started in Armagh. Many of the screws were bad bastards but there were some honest ones who would wonder how it had all come to this, though the answer was no mystery to us.

We had crystal sets to listen to the news but the prisoners who still had political status would shout over to us and we also all met up at Mass on Sundays which was when we got supplied with tobacco and cigarette papers.

During the summer of 1980 the question kept getting asked, what's next? It was sort of inevitable that the only other avenue we had was to hunger strike. So, we talked and talked about it. Mairead Farrell, our Officer Commanding, was in contact with the OC in the H-Blocks and we knew they were talking about it as well.

The time came for people to volunteer. I thought long and hard about it but couldn't just think about myself. My father was sick and still hadn't got over losing my mammy. I had to think of my brothers. But I was very, very determined and I wasn't expecting someone else to do what I wasn't prepared to do. So, I put my name down. It wasn't done lightly. Wasn't just a rash decision. I was almost twenty-five so I think I was mature enough. I said to myself, there's every possibility I will die. It wasn't a case of, Ach, we'll be on it a few weeks and Margaret Thatcher will give in. I was never under that impression.

The leadership didn't want the hunger strike and they sent in all this information about what it can do to you, your body and vital organs. They tried to deter us.

The men went on hunger strike on 27 October. Mairead Farrell, Margaret Nugent and myself joined them on 1 December.

That morning we began, the screws put Mairead, Margaret and myself in a double cell together. The cell was never without food. They took away breakfast and replaced it with lunch. Took away lunch and replaced it with supper, etc. Jail food is notoriously rotten and cold – fat with a bit of meat through it. But all of a sudden, the plates were overflowing with steaming hot chips that smelt so appetising.

A screw would say, "Those chips have been counted, so we'll know if you're eating."

They were taking blood samples every day and weighing us and would have known if we were eating. They were so petty.

We were advised to take salt diluted in the water and to drink about eight pints a day. That first night I was as sick as a dog, throwing up.

Going into the second week they moved us to the so-called hospital wing and you had to have a bath. We hadn't washed in ten months. We were secretly looking forward to a hot bath but the whole pleasure was taken out of it because we felt so weak and it drained us further.

Cardinal Ó Fiaich came into see us and brought us cigarettes. Fr Murray was a brilliant chaplain and without him there were times when I didn't know what we would have done. He fought for us more so than most of the Catholic Church who let us down very badly. Had they done more the second hunger strike would never have taken place.

In mid-December we knew that Sean McKenna, who was on hunger strike in the H-Blocks, was very ill. We were listening to the nine o'clock news one night and quickly looked at each other: had we heard right? The hunger strike was over? We were glued, waiting for the ten o'clock news and when it was confirmed we thought our demands had been met. We said, "Thank God, for the sake of Sean McKenna and his family that the Brits have seen sense and recognised us for what we are."

But then we were paranoid: what if they were just saying that on the radio. So, we decided to keep on the hunger strike. The next morning the screws once again brought in breakfast, cornflakes and mugs of tea, and told us the hunger strike was over. Mairead said, "We're still on it."

The governor came in and said that if we were calling it off, "not to be eating that food", meaning the breakfast. Mairead came back from a visit and confirmed the news and so we ended our hunger strike after nineteen days. A few days later we were sent back to the wing to join the rest of the comrades.

My daddy had been 110% behind me but he couldn't come up during the hunger strike – it was too much for him. He came up when it was over and you should have seen the relief on his face. He was the happiest man on earth.

As the days went on it was such a kick in the stomach when we realised that the Brits had reneged on their promises. We were angry. Then there was talk of a second hunger strike. We discussed it and Mairead and I decided to put our names forward again.

Then I began to think about it, more and more. You don't realise what you're putting your family through and I decided I couldn't put my family through it again. So I withdrew my name and then Mairead said that she had also reconsidered and would not be taking part. Some of the other prisoners – some serving short sentences – volunteered, but in the end there was to be no second hunger strike in Armagh. We didn't have large numbers to draw from, like in the Blocks.

For both of us it was an agonising decision because the women were always a part of the prison struggle. We just weren't "wee girls", the way some referred to us. I had been writing to Bobby Sands regularly and I remember getting a comm from him. He said that when he heard there wasn't going to be a hunger strike in Armagh he was the happiest man in Long Kesh. He didn't mean it chauvinistically, but comradely, affectionately.

Along with the men, we simultaneously ended the no wash/no slop out protest. We were still locked up all day but were allowed out at night and were able to watch the news on television.

When Bobby went on hunger strike, we had mixed emotions – pride, terror but, above all, a sense of helplessness. We intensified the writing campaign, lobbying across the world. His election victory gave us a real buzz. We convinced ourselves that this would lead to talks and a resolution of the protest but it didn't.

In the last days of his hunger strike you were trying to stay continually awake, as if you were on watch. That Monday night I was exhausted and fell asleep. The screws quietly opened the doors at 7.30 the next morning. There was an eerie silence throughout the wing. I went to slop out and in the toilets Brenda Murphy came in and said, "Did you hear..."

I knew by the expression on her face.

"Bobby died this morning..."

I went back to my cell and just broke my heart. Even though we were expecting it from the reports of how he was deteriorating, it was still unreal. That night we saw the scenes on the news, his poor mother and father. It was so sad but we were so angry that it made us more determined even though we were totally frustrated at having no means to express our anger.

It never got easier, after each hunger striker died. It tore you apart.

It was a Saturday and I was just called for a visit when I learnt that the hunger strike was over. After seven long months it was over. We all cried. I was relieved that no more comrades would be dying. I was relieved for their families. But I thought of the families of the ten men who had died and how they must be feeling.

It seems it happened only yesterday. The feelings are still raw. And then, after it ended, we got our demands, slowly but surely.

Unless you have been in jail you cannot understand the bond between comrades. I don't mean that we were anything special. It's just hard to explain that we were all there for one another. I had my down days, especially after my mammy was murdered. My comrades helped me through and I would have been lost without them. I never had sisters but there are some of those women whom even if I had had a sister, I couldn't have been closer to. ■

After her release from prison Mary married former IRA prisoner Terence (Cleaky) Clark who escaped from prison twice. They had two children. After his release Terence became head of Gerry Adams' security team while Mary was elected to Belfast City Hall as a Sinn Féin Councillor.

I was Part of the 2000 Mass Hunger Strike

Mansour Atif Rayan
Palestine

MY name is Mansour Atif Rayan, I am from the village of Qarawat Bani Hassan, west of Nablus. I was arrested on the 2 April, 1993 and sentenced to life and twenty years imprisonment.

I was released as part of the prisoner swap deal in 2011, when the Israeli soldier Gilad Shalit was freed by Hamas in exchange for 1,027 Palestine prisoners.

During the years of my imprisonment, I participated in all the hunger strikes that took place in Israeli occupation prisons, most notably the 2000 and the 2004 mass hunger strikes.

I wrote a book, *The Diaries of a Prisoner on Hunger Strike*, about those protests.

In planning a hunger strike, it can take up to a year or two for Palestinian prisoners to make a decision to use a hunger strike as a last resort.

Strikes are organised to put pressure on the administration of the Israeli Prison Service (IPS) to meet the demands of the prisoners.

All of these demands are already guaranteed by international law, which ensures prisoners' rights, including those classified as security prisoners.

Written plans on future strikes are passed from prison to prison, either by capsules carried by inmates or through lawyers.

The 2000 mass hunger strike was a big one.

The plan was to start a strike, which included all prisons in occupied Palestine from Alsabaa and Nafha in the south, to Hadarim in the north and Ashkelon in the middle. The prisoners' leadership negotiated with the Israeli Prison Service to achieve three demands. 1. The release of about 50 prisoners in solitary confinement including inmates who had spent ten years there. 2. Allowing prisoners to access university courses by mail. 3. The right for prisoners to have phone contact with their families. The decision to begin the strike came after the prison administration refused our legitimate demands.

Hunger strikes are a battle of fire and iron. We began ours by storing salt so our stomachs would not rot from the lack of food.

We kept radios to follow up with the media coverage of the strike.

A very important point when prisoners are considering starting a hunger strike is the outside world: the more peaceful the global political situation, the more ready the world tends to be to receive news of a strike and to engage, taking it to the forefront of media coverage.

This increases the ability of international institutions, especially the International Committee of the Red Cross (ICRC) to pressure the Israeli Occupation to meet our demands.

Some of the sick prisoners were exempted from taking part in the strike, but to show their determination they decided to participate, knowing that they could possibly die, particularly those suffering from diabetes, blood pressure and stomach ulcers.

I witnessed how they started writing their wills and letters of farewell to their wives, children and families in case they died.

Our motto was either death or fulfilment of our demands, so the strike was a matter of life or death. Our insistence on winning our demands was amazing.

A few days into the strike the IPS began transferring prisoners who lost consciousness and other ill inmates to the prison clinic, where they were given paracetamol or painkillers.

I saw patients being thrown from medical stretchers to the ground by officers. Imagine a weak patient, on hunger strike for weeks, suffering from diabetes with a shrunken stomach or no longer able to speak, being thrown from a stair and his body left on the ground.

This brutal treatment was to pressure sick prisoners and other inmates to end their strike.

The news coverage began as soon as we started our hunger strike and the media began to react. Silence spread throughout the jail. Prisoners were determined to achieve their just demands.

After the first twenty days of the protest had passed, I saw how the strikers' bodies were getting weaker, but they kept repeating, "Achieve our demands or death." Newspapers, radio and TV stations carried stories and news of the strike.

Because the Israeli occupation was afraid of exposing its criminal nature and its violations of international law, along with prisoners' rights, the occupation authorities approached the prisoners' leadership of the strike to negotiate a deal.

The leadership refused to talk to the prison authorities.

The Israeli Prison Service appeared to fear the possibility of a scandal, if prisoners died while on hunger strike.

Prisoners negotiated with Shin Bet (the Israeli secret service) itself.

Avi Dichter, former Shin Bet director, came and spoke with us about our demands which were met after thirty days of strike action.

Media coverage and support from the Palestinian people for our strike played the most important role in the success of the 2000 strike. ■

Mansour Atif Rayan is a 44-year-old former Palestinian political prisoner. He spent nineteen years in Israeli jails and was released in October 2011 as part of the Shalit swap deal. He was deported from Salfit city in the West Bank and currently lives in the Gaza Strip.

Room Number Four

Thaer Mahmoud Al-Kurd
Palestine

I AM the freed prisoner Thaer Mahmoud Al-Kurd from
Jabalyia refugee camp.

I took part in an open-ended hunger strike during my
detention, which extended from 8 August, 1988 until I was
released twenty-three years later in the Gilad Shalit prisoner
exchange deal in 2011.

Even after my release, the horrors of that strike and my
time in prison haunt me constantly and have impacted on
my life.

The decision to engage in my first hunger strike came in
1991. That strike lasted sixteen days. At the time none of the
senior inmates informed me of what I needed to do.

A week before the strike I could not sleep well, as my mind was concentrating on the upcoming protest.

The goal of that hunger strike was to obtain access to food necessary to sustain life, from the prison canteen and to be allowed more family visits.

The strike began in Nafha jail, where prisoners suffered badly in the heat of the very hot summer of 1991.

The prison authorities would not allow electric fans to cool the air in the cells. Unbearably stifling high temperatures caused psychological pressures, which took their toll on the men.

Our bodies were pumping sweat, and we appealed to the prison administration to allow fans, but they refused.

United Nations rules insist on humane conditions for every prisoner in jails all over the world, yet we suffered in the stifling hell of an Israeli-occupation prison.

When I joined the hunger strike, no one warned me about the danger of weakness and that if I wanted to stand up, I should rise very slowly. Attempting to stand on the third day I suddenly felt dizzy and everything in the room was spinning.

For two full days I hadn't eaten any food, only water with salt. My feeble body hit the ground and I went into a coma that lasted hours.

The occupation authorities expected me to declare an end to my strike and lead my fellow strikers to give up, but I resisted and continued my protest.

I was among 280 prisoners in four sections of the jail: A, B, C and D, where the majority of the prisoners, except for the sick patients, were on hunger strike.

The aims of the strike were to achieve basic demands: fans in our cells; family visits from Gaza and the West Bank and to increase the Foura: the time prisoners are let out of their cells to exercise in an open area.

Despite everything, that strike failed. The next one in 1992 was an important success. The failure of the first strike was caused by the lack of participation by all prisons, coordination between prisons was not as good as it could have been.

In the 1991 strike, Nafha prison took action alone without having good media coverage.

1992 saw the unification of prisoners which forced the authorities to comply with our demands.

Hunger strikes take a long time to organise and coordinate.

The success or failure of a strike I believe, lies in the extent of the media coverage it receives.

The fact that starting a hunger strike is a difficult step, not taken lightly. But hunger has never been a huge burden to prisoners, who see the battle for justice as a major cause worth fighting for.

For me, I had spent sixteen days on hunger strike with severe pains in all the joints and limbs of my body. Even after the strike ended, for months I suffered problems with my digestive system.

So, as you can see the decision to go on a hunger strike is not an easy one. It is harder than imprisonment itself. ■

Thaer Mahmoud Al-Kurd is a 50-year-old former Palestinian political prisoner who works as a freelancer. He spent twenty four years in Israeli jails and was released in October 2011 as part of the Shalit swap deal. He lives in the Gaza Strip.

The Unified Strike and Its Martyrs

Fouad Kassem Al-Razim
Palestine

I AM liberated prisoner Fouad Kassim Razim from Jerusalem. I was sentenced and spent thirty-one consecutive years in jail. I am sixty-three years old and married. I was released in the "Promise of the Free" Prisoner Swap Deal (The 2011 Shalit Deal) and deported to the Gaza Strip.

My first experience with staging a hunger strike was in 1981 in Ramle prison.

First off, back then, we had given the prisoners several days' notice of the strike to allow them to attend Friday prayers and to avoid the intervention of the authorities.

Then there was an assault by the jail authorities on the worshippers during the Friday prayers.

That was at the beginning of the 1981 hunger strike, which was my first experience of the protests which also took place in 1984, 1987 and 1992.

I want to tell you about the most successful hunger strike in the history of the prisoners' national movement in Israeli jails. It happened in 1992 when we as prisoners benefited and built on the experiences of previous strikes.

The secret of the success of that strike, which had been planned for three consecutive years, was the participation of all prisons and prisoners.

A specific strike date was agreed on, it began in the Junaid prison in Nablus and was gradually joined by all prisons.

Starting in the central prison of Junaid, the protest then incorporated Ashkelon, Beersheba and Nafha.

The strike was soon joined by the rest of the prisons. Two weeks later, sick inmates and those who didn't take part initially in the strike also joined.

We imposed our agenda on the occupation authorities and they filled nearly all our demands, except the requirement to allow prisoners take part in Arab university courses by mail.

In the 1992 strike we had many achievements, most important was: the recognition of prisoner representation with the authorities in the jails; the introduction of electric fans in the cells and the supply of winter bedding and clothing.

We also achieved our demands for the so called 'tile', which functions on electricity and is also used to boil and cook food.

The most important humane achievement was allowing prisoners to see their children, who up until then were deprived of visiting their parents in prison.

Duration of family visits was extended from thirty to forty-five minutes and twice monthly visits were allowed.

The authorities also agreed to family visits during holidays.

The hunger strike's success also led to the improvement in the quality and quantity of goods sold in the prison shop, such as grocery and soft drinks.

They also agreed to allow prisoners to join the Hebrew University where prisoners began to study by mail.

When the Israeli Prison Service (IPS) found out about this action, they immediately prevented the move as they didn't want Palestinian prisoners to be educated.

During the 1992 strike, the confrontation with the occupation was collective and the prison authorities were unable to impose their arbitrary rule on us.

Prisoners were not transferred to other prisons and cells because all of the inmates were on hunger strike.

Up to that period they routinely moved hunger strikers to prisons that didn't take part in the protests, which was not the case in the 1992 hunger strike.

During the 2000 strike I was transferred from jail to jail, Nafha to Ishel. I was placed in a cell with only one other inmate. Our cell was isolated from the rest of cells in the prison. The guards burst in on us several times a day and tried to force me to end my hunger strike.

The prison service moved my cell-mate to another jail. All along the prison's director, an intelligence officer, was pressuring me psychologically by telling me I was isolated and I couldn't hear the news of the strikes.

He insisted that, "All prisoners have broken their strikes. You are the only one who remains on hunger strike."

He tried to play with my mind because I was one of the leaders of the 2000 strike. But I always repeated, "Death or fulfilment of our legitimate demands."

Our bodies were weak and thin, we couldn't even stand. They moved us between cells to increase our exhaustion and refused to give us salt for two weeks. Prisoners' stomachs began to rot as a result of the lack of salt until they returned it to us after they realised that we were going to strike until the very end.

One of their biggest problems was the fear as the health of a prisoner deteriorated significantly and they approached death.

The Israeli Prison Service was trying to bargain with us, being leaders of the strike, by saying that they were ready to provide treatment for the prisoners in exchange for the end of the protest.

In the aftermath of the strike, the IPS didn't provide us with fluids, like soup or milk, which would have made absorption of solid food easier.

Nothing was done to help inmates return to normal health. Many prisoners would go on to suffer from gastrointestinal tract complaints.

In 1992, prisoner Hussein Nimer Abayat, who was on hunger strike in Ashkelon prison with us, passed away.

Two prisoners, Ali Al-Jaafari and Rasim Halawah, were martyred in the 1980 strikes. Prisoner Mahmoud Fritikh was martyred too, at the Junaid prison near Nablus in 1984. ■

Fouad Kassem Al-Razim is a 63-year-old former Palestinian political prisoner who is married with three children and is now retired. He spent thirty one years in Israeli jails and was released in October 2011 as part of the Shalit swap deal. He was deported from Jerusalem and currently lives in the Gaza Strip.

Hunger Strike: The Last Battle of the Prisoner

Mohamed Abdel Karim Abuataya
Palestine

I SPENT nineteen years of my life in Israeli jails, imprisoned first in 1992. I am now forty-years old. I left prison as part of the Shalit Deal in 2011.

The experience of a hunger strike is difficult, because refraining from taking food is called passive resistance by the prisoners, in which the jailer is forced to confront the prisoners until their demands, like the improvement of living conditions, are met.

It is an opportunity for inmates to put pressure on the jailer to respond to the just rights of prisoners.

Over the years of Israeli occupation, hunger strikes have helped us prisoners to improve many of the conditions we live under.

Our struggle entails a great deal of suffering, especially when it's the first experience of a prisoner taking on a hunger strike.

During my strikes I have lost a lot of weight, I have suffered stress and quite a few medical ailments, particularly later in life.

I took part in three hunger strike battles, each a completely different experience. The initial one was very difficult because it was my first.

Veteran prisoners always gave us moral support and instructions as how to deal with the strikes.

I engaged in another hunger strike while in solitary confinement and I found its complications exceptionally painful.

During the first days, my weight dropped rapidly, losing about eight kilos in the first week.

After three days I found myself sluggish. A short while after, my hair began to fall out. I was weak and had to endure aches and pains in my arms, legs and back, to the extent that I could not stand.

This was added to by the psychological pressure we were constantly subjected to by our jailers, such as allowing families of common criminal Israeli inmates to bring in meat, vegetables, fruits and spices to be cooked by the prisoners.

They would grill meat so that the aroma of appetising food would drift through to the cells of us hunger strikers.

We had to bear so much to achieve our demands.

After that hunger strike, which lasted up to 30 days, my fellow prisoners and I had difficulty getting back to regular health.

We had to return gradually to everyday living. Any mistakes by inmates, like eating directly, caused stomach ulcers, haemorrhoids or renal failure, because our digestive systems had been damaged throughout the strike period.

I will never forget how even simple food felt like concrete in my stomach. Aching joints and back pains were constant. Knowing this, the jailers used to hit my spine and back intentionally.

Hunger strikes can be a personal or collective decision and whoever decides to fight a personal hunger strike has the right to do so. In one situation for me it was a personal choice.

I once took a decision in solitary confinement to mount a hunger strike, to achieve certain demands and I succeeded in achieving my goal three days later. As for the collective decision to engage in a strike, the best time of the year are the months of April, May, September and October because of the moderate temperatures.

When it came to collective hunger strikes, decisions would only be taken to start action after the exhaustion of all options and dialogue with the Israeli Prison Service not reaching a positive resolution.

In one situation we engaged in a hunger strike after talking to all the inmates, and the results of the discussions were presented to the prisoners' leadership group who decided collectively what to do.

The more prisoners are unified under one leadership the better the chances of the hunger strike to succeed.

It's a fact also that when a prisoner breaks his hunger strike suddenly, he affects the morale of the rest of the strikers in the protest.

A united hunger strike causes fear among the Israeli occupation, especially when it exposes the fact that they are not meeting the basic demands of the prisoners and their rights, in front of international organisations.

Our demands have always been and will always be in keeping with humanitarian laws. ■

Mohamed Abdel Karim Abuataya is a 52-year-old former Palestinian political prisoner. He is married and has six daughters. He spent over nineteen years in Israeli jails and was released in October 2011 as part of the Shalit prisoners swap. He lives in the Gaza Strip.

The Night & I

Khalil Abu Aram

The night and I are alone.
The full moon
and the dull eyes of my cell-mates
are windows.

I am with my coffee,
sleeplessness,
cigarette
and smoke.

My thoughts – delirious – swirl and rove
from ascension to fall
– while my companions snore.

Eyes that do not sleep;
the night swarming, thronging;
a life intolerable,
a yearning for freedom...

But death is not the answer.
No, by Allah! That will not be the answer.

Our day makes us weary,
motion... screaming, clamour;
its light is darkness!

This is not the end we want,
not now, not ever.

Our gatherings have become graves,
their living, victims,
our jailers, whores,
our enemy, bitter – and cowards.
They bare us their teeth,
and their poison is bile, is venom.

How neat and trimly dressed.
At times, civil in speech,
and at times,
they play their parts.

We were not created for this.
No man was created for this.

The Creator marked us out for honour,
fashioned us and perfected our being.

Our courtyards have become the enemy's pasture.
Our ignorance profits them.
Our discord is debasement.

Would that we rose from the slumber that afflicts us,
and from dreams turned to fantasy.
Everyone of us is absent or disappeared,
mindless or bewildered.

Is this how we are?
Is this our fault
or the fault of destiny?
Or is the fault in our poor choices?

So, nation of Yasir and Yasin!
People of Palestine, every one of you!
Where is our harmony?
For unity and oneness will always be
the vessels of peace.

Be free, be independent.
Let there be no collision, no quarrel!

You are the soldiers of fury,
The salt of the earth,
the unwavering challenge.
Reclaim the pages of honour.
Its lines are glory.

Mothers and families of Palestinian prisoners stage a sit-in demonstration in solidarity with hunger striker Bilal Kayid.

Imprisoned in the Republic of Ireland

Martin Ferris
Ireland

OUR comrades in British-controlled jails in the North of Ireland had won political status in 1972 – before it was later withdrawn, a decision which led to the loss of many lives.

But the government in the South of Ireland also played a role in suppressing the republican struggle by collaborating with the British authorities, passing on intelligence and imprisoning hundreds of activists over the years of the conflict. Mountjoy Prison, Portlaoise Prison and Limerick Prison – which had witnessed protests including the deaths of hunger strikers in earlier periods of struggle (1920s, 1940s) – were to witness similar protests from 1969 onwards, until prisoners were released under the 1998 Good Friday Agreement.

The authorities had recognised IRA command structures for a time but, like the British, reneged on previous agreements. In Portlaoise they attempted to break the IRA. Any prisoner who refused to be strip-searched was placed in solitary confinement. They also demanded the strip-searching of family members. For almost twelve months until March 1977 many POWs spent that entire period in solitary confinement without any contact with their families or comrades.

It became clear that nothing short of a hunger strike would be needed to highlight the intolerable conditions inside the prison and force the administration to change its policy. In the past there had always been dialogue and negotiations between the prisoners' Officer Commanding and the prison governor – even when dates had been set for a hunger strike. With such channels of communication there was always some chance of resolution to the problem. On this occasion, however, the governor's policy was to sever contact and he ignored the prisoners' representatives. In this type of atmosphere confrontation is a foregone conclusion.

An earlier hunger strike in Portlaoise in 1975 had been resolved but not before the health of one of the prisoners, Pat Ward, was permanently damaged. Pat never recovered full use of his speech and the hunger strike contributed to his early death.

Hunger strikes as a form of prison protest is never contemplated lightly. To use one's own body as both the weapon and the battle ground is something that is only considered as a last resort. So many things had to be taken into account and weighed up before the decision to embark on a hunger strike is taken. Each man had to ask himself were conditions so intolerable that he would be willing, nay – forced – to adopt this course of action? Could he deal with the anguish, the excruciating pain, the physical and the physiological pressure it would inevitably bring to bear on not alone himself but his family? Had he the will power, once the fast began, to see it through to the very painful end, to die if necessary? Would he lay down his life for his principles and comrades? Did a hunger strike have a chance of success?

Questions such as these weighed heavily on the minds of the prisoners. It was not an easy decision to make. Reluctantly the prisoners answered a hushed 'Yes' to themselves to each of these questions.

In order to maximise the chances of a hunger strike succeeding it is necessary to build a public awareness campaign around the issues involved and hopefully generate sympathy and support behind those taking part in the protest. Because of restrictions on visits, censorship of letters in the prison, censorship in the media outside and a generally subservient and unsympathetic press, it had not been possible to promote awareness and focus public attention on the worsening situation inside the prison.

The political climate was another factor which militated against their chances of success. An atmosphere of fear had gripped the country under the pro-British coalition government in Dublin. The introduction of 'a state of emergency' and the Emergency Powers Act gave the Gardai (police) extraordinary powers. Anyone arrested could be interrogated for up to seven days. A special department of the police – who became known as 'the heavy gang' – used torture and beatings to force detainees to sign confessions. The government also banned Irish republicans from celebrating the sixtieth anniversary of the 1916 Rising, although republicans celebrated anyway outside the GPO in Dublin where the Rising had started.

A government attempt to introduce widespread censorship was opposed. However, the press in general, with a few notable exceptions, did surrender to governmental pressure and turned a blind eye to the abuses of power, particularly towards prisoners.

IRA prisoners discussed their position long and hard and expressed their doubts and fears. So desperate had the situation become, however, that to allow conditions to continue as they were without confronting them as a unit would almost certainly lead to individuals taking things into their own hands. In any case the prisoners knew that stepping back now would only serve to postpone the inevitable and prolong the agony of the suffering prisoners. Reluctantly, the IRA within the prison sanctioned the hunger strike. The IRA leadership outside were informed of the decision and tried in vain to persuade the prisoners to abandon this course of action.

On 6 March, 1977, twenty IRA prisoners, including myself, began refusing food. Two of the hunger strikers, Kevin Mallon and Daithi O Conaill, were also designated as negotiators with the power and authority to agree terms for ending the fast. The central demand was for a public enquiry into conditions inside the prison. It was hoped such an enquiry would lead to a general improvement in conditions. Ten days after the fast began the governor had the twenty hunger strikers moved to one side of E1 landing. Conditions similar to those in solitary confinement were imposed. Technically, the prisoners were in breach of the prison rules by refusing food. This was to be the first time, in this phase of the struggle, that fasting prisoners in the South of Ireland were deliberately isolated for the duration of the fast. They received no letters, visits, radio, papers, or cigarettes, and were locked up for twenty-three hours a day.

To reach the exercise yard and returning from it every day the other prisoners had to pass through E1 landing. To prevent them from communicating with the fasting prisoners a Prison Officer and Gardai were placed outside each of the cell doors containing the hunger striker. In the exercise yard the same tactic was employed. Gardai and Prison Officers were in position outside the cell windows in an attempt to deny prisoners any contact, verbal or otherwise.

Every day, meals were placed in the hunger strikers' cells as a matter of course and left there for the entire twenty-four hours. The idea behind these tactics was simple: isolate the prisoners, deny them the solace, comfort and support of their comrades, and gradually weaken their resolve to continue on the fast. The food, too, would both be an added temptation and the fulfilling of the authorities' legal responsibility to provide sustenance to those in their custody. They put extra portions on each plate to emphasise the point.

As the hunger strike progressed the men's resistance to the cold weakened. E1 landing is located on the ground floor and is one of the coldest landings in the block. A request to the governor for the hunger strikers to be moved to either the E2 or E3 landings was denied. The prison doctor while agreeing with the prisoners' request on medical grounds was not prepared to exert his influence. Were he to insist on the move the governor would have no other option but to comply.

A few members of the Visiting Committee visited a couple of the hunger strikers in their cells. They showed little compassion and even less interest in the prisoners' plight. Their only function, it seemed, was to repeat and emphasise the governor and the government's line on the fast, which was to inform the prisoners that the hunger strike would not succeed, their demands would not be met. Prison management could depend on the collaboration and support of so-called independent bodies as always.

Some of the local priests did visit hunger strikers and gave them the sacraments in being cells. They expressed understanding, sympathy and concern. However, they were not prepared to comment publicly. Fasting prisoners who wished to and were able to climb the stairs to attend prison mass in the chapel did so. Like those in solitary before them, however, they too were herded into a purpose-built wire cage segregating them from their comrades. Even in the sanctuary of the chapel not a gesture of compassion was forthcoming.

After twenty-five days, with their condition weakening at various rates, the authorities began to transfer some of the hunger strikers to the Curragh Military Hospital.

By the thirty-second day they had all been transferred. On leaving the prison, despite being weak and having been isolated from contact with their comrades, the prisoners were forcibly strip searched. The same procedure was employed when they arrived at the Curragh Military Hospital. Here again the prisoners were strip searched even though their only contact was with their jailers. It was a blatant attempt to punish and degrade the prisoners in the hope that it would break their will to continue on the fast.

One prisoner in particular, Kevin Mallon, because he resisted the strip search, was handcuffed to the hospital bed in retaliation. The handcuffs were only removed when a medical orderly intervened. All this was meant as an example to the other prisoners on the fast. There would be no kid-glove treatment here, no sympathy. Security once more remained of paramount importance.

Outside the prison growing concern for the plight of the prisoners was manifesting itself in public support. A mass demonstration was held in Portlaoise in early April. The demonstrators began to converge on the prison but short of their destination they found their way blocked by the garda riot squad, with heavily armed soldiers and special branch detectives in reserve. As the demonstrators approached the cordon the garda riot squad swung into action and baton-charged the crowd. Those who were able fought back and some fierce hand-to-hand fighting erupted. However, the gardai were well equipped with batons, helmets with visors and heavy clothing. The protesters had little chance of fighting against this well-organised, well-protected and vicious force. The crowd began to scatter in all directions as the garda onslaught continued. Anyone caught in their way was given 'the timber' and bludgeoned to the ground. Neither age nor youth was considered. No one was spared. Frail old men and women got the same treatments as the youths caught by the police. Many of the protesters were seriously injured, some with serious head wounds.

One of the protesters, Sean Brosnan, from Dingle, County Kerry, who was in his fifties at the time, suffered severe head injuries. Shortly afterwards Brosnan was to fall victim to a serious stroke, attributed to the police beating, which confined him to a wheelchair for the remainder of his life. Many of those who received bad beatings had been a considerable distance from the disturbances and couldn't possibly have constituted a threat of any kind.

Further protest marches in Dublin and throughout the country passed off peacefully. Public support continued to grow as people became more aware of the deplorable and inhuman conditions within the prison. Influential people of conscience began to take an active role. Bishop James Kavanagh of Dublin along with Senator Michael Mullen, General Secretary of a major trade union, attempted to promote negotiations. The government's public position was uncompromising. There would be no concessions to the hunger-strikers' demands. Bishop Kavanagh visited the Curragh Military Hospital and met with both O Conaill and Mallon on the thirty-ninth day of the strike.

After forty days two of the prisoners ended their fast, followed by four more over the next few days. After forty-five days without food the remaining fourteen hunger strikers were finally allowed a visit. Understandably, this was a very emotional and traumatic moment for the prisoners and their families who were meeting each other for the first time since the fast began. The steadfast and unbending support received from the families was of enormous comfort to the fourteen men who were determined to continue with their fast.

The hunger strike ended on the forty-seventh day after a second visit from Bishop Kavanagh. The bishop brought a message from Michael Mullen which contained the basis for a settlement of the hunger strike. The prisoners were led to believe that the proposal for a settlement was known to and recommended by the republican leadership outside. The prisoners were assured that 'influential people associated with the government, and, in particular, the main opposition party, Fianna Fáil party, had guaranteed that once the prisoners ended their fast there would be almost immediate improvements in conditions.'

When we ended their fast, we did so in the belief that core issues would be addressed. However, the government said that they had faced down the hunger strike and offered no concessions. Conditions did improve, albeit slowly. The improvements helped to ease some of the pressures in the prison. The governor recognised IRA structures. Abolition of the infamous and degrading body searches followed shortly afterwards. Also discontinued were some of the petty restrictions placed on prisoners. The over-supervision of family visits was relaxed and the cage was removed from the chapel.

A few short weeks after the ending of the hunger strike the coalition government was destroyed in a general election. The two ministers, Conor Cruise O'Brien and Paddy Cooney, who were the public faces of the draconian government suffered personal defeats, losing their seats. Fianna Fáil swept to power, elected with an unprecedented majority. The Portlaoise hunger strike played a major role in bringing about the downfall of the coalition government, highlighting as it did the brutal nature of the regime and its virulent anti-republican and anti-nationalist policies.

Shortly after the new Fianna Fáil government took office the editors of the three national daily papers were invited into the prison to view for themselves the prevailing conditions. The Irish Press editor, Tim Pat Coogan, in his book, The IRA, wrote that tensions still remained. There were sixteen uniformed gardai patrolling the floor of each landing. He also spoke about families being left standing in all types of weather outside the prison waiting to be allowed in to visit. Often visits were denied to people after travelling long distances. The most degrading and detested practice of strip searching, which some prisoners endured many times in one day, was still carried out. Some prison officers and justice officers told him that they were under orders 'to ensure that the Provisionals (the IRA) were confronted at every hand's turn when the familiar republican defiance of prison regulations began'.

Of the twenty prisoners who embarked on the 1977 hunger strike five died prematurely, no doubt due to the effects of their forty-seven days on the strike. ∎

Martin Ferris was imprisoned on three occasions, twice on IRA membership charges, and later received a ten-year sentence when he was caught by the Irish navy, off the coast of Ireland, on a boat, the Marita Ann, importing seven tonnes of explosives and arms. After his release he stood for election to the Irish parliament and topped the poll in North Kerry. He stood down from parliament in 2020.

The Sound of Eating Carrots Amidst Hunger Strikers

Walid Mahmoud Miqdad
Palestine

I AM freed prisoner Walid Mahmoud Miqdad. I'm fifty-three years old, married with a son and daughter, I live in Al-Shari refugee camp, west of Gaza City.

I was detained for a total of four and a half years. Every day while in prison I was in conflict with the administration of the Israeli Prison Service (IPS).

They were always trying to make prisoners' lives miserable and did everything possible to add to our hardship, even taking away our electric fans.

We used the fans to cool our cells in the middle of blazing hot summers and heating them in the cold chill of winters.

We also used the fans for cooking food.

The IPS would use punishments like depriving us of blankets to keep warm in winter. They also reduced the quality and quantity of our food rations, leading us to fear for our health and well-being.

Though wounded and in constant need of medication, the administration placed me along with other sick inmates in a separate unit with hunger strikers.

Knowing we were ill and needing food, it was distressing for us and the hungers strikers as we were being fed.

It was clear their vile psychological strategy was to torment us and the hunger strikers by choosing the best quality food for us to eat, as the strikers starved in pain and agony.

We were ashamed to eat in front of the striking prisoners.

They were suffering extreme hunger due to many long days of not taking food.

Once they brought us carrots as part of their psychological war. We were embarrassed to eat them in front of the strikers, because the crunching sounds of the carrots being chewed would have been unbearable for them to hear.

Some of the ill prisoners would go under their covers to eat their carrots, so as not to make any sounds.

I was ashamed and refused to eat foods which when being eaten would upset the strikers.

It is known that on a hunger protest the striker's saliva becomes bitter to taste. Knowing this the guards would pass through the prison and tempt strikers with bottles of orange juice and Coca-Cola to quench the bitterness in their mouths.

The hunger strikers would be adamant and refuse the temptation, continue their strike and maintain their dignity.

The biggest agony of prison life was not seeing our children. The administration would sometimes deny family visits. They only allowed face-to-face visits for fifteen minutes, yet after one hunger strike victory we were allowed to see our children for forty-five minutes every month.

They also gave permission for prisoners to sit with their children, prior to visits from older family members.

Before the changes, the inmate had a barrier between himself and his visitors. It meant that he and his family or friends were only allowed phone contact to communicate with each other, through a grimy barrier.

I remember twenty-five years ago when prisoners stopped meeting their families in protest at the short period allowed for visits.

There was always great sorrow in the eyes of married prisoners, especially those sentenced to life, at not seeing their children.

Prisoners sacrificed their dearest longing in life, in order to achieve better prison conditions and more access to their families.

Their demands were finally granted, following repeated hunger strikes.

By sheer will and determination, they attained many of their legitimate demands by refraining from taking food and through challenging their jailers, in their battle for human rights. ∎

Walid Mahmoud Miqdad is a former Palestinian political prisoner who heads the prisoners' affairs department of a prisoner group. He currently resides in the Gaza Strip.

Palestinian young men hold banners that read 'salt and water' to show solidarity with Palestinian prisoners on hunger strike in Israeli jails.

The Closure of the Cruel Rats' Section

Zuhair Salah Al-Chechnya
Palestine

I AM freed prisoner Zuhair Salah Al-Chechnya from Bureij refugee camp in the middle of the Gaza Strip. I belong to Fatah. I was sentenced to life and spent twenty-two years in jail until 2011. I was released under the 2011 Shalit Deal. I am fifty-years-old and married with three daughters.

In 1990, with two daughters and another on the way, I was imprisoned and by the time I was freed in 2011, my three grown-up daughters were married.

Being in jail I missed many happy years watching my girls grow up, time I will never get back.

I consider hunger striking to be one of the most difficult weapons used by a prisoner to resist the conditions of his detention.

A hunger protest is a double-edged sword.

Prisoners don't resort to these hunger protests unless all roads and solutions to extract their rights from the prison administration are exhausted.

At the beginning, the occupation adopted a policy of detention that attempted to empty the Palestinian fighter of any revolutionary spirit by sentencing prisoners to long sentences.

It wanted to tear apart Palestinian society by dispersing all the detainees away from their families.

I took part in my first hunger strike in 1992. We did all in our power to fight our battle by corresponding with the responsible authorities of the occupation including the Israeli Prison Service (IPS) as well as the office of the Israeli Prime Minister.

Although all our demands were legal and legitimate, we didn't receive a positive response and decided to go on hunger strike.

We began by drinking only water with salt, in a bid to use our stomachs in the battle to win our rights.

I went on six consecutive strikes, the most significant of which was the successful 1992 hunger strike, where we won the right to have our children visit and to be allowed electric cooling fans in our cells during summertime.

I was advised against taking part in that strike because I was suffering from Behçet's disease, but despite my illnesses

I decided to go on hunger strike anyway.

In one of the strikes I suffered from serious ill-health and was transferred to Ramle prison for three days.

There the IPS started bargaining with me, trying to persuade me to abandon the strike, for fear of me losing my life.

They talked around the clock, telling me to halt my protest.

I told the IPS, "If you really fear for my life, you'll have to meet our legal and humanitarian demands."

The most important achievement of that strike was the ending of solitary confinement, which we won by battling with our blood and health.

What had been happening was that some prisoners had been put into tiny cells alone in isolation for many years, this would affect their health and mental wellbeing, also causing permanent suffering, well into their later lives.

The 'section of rats' issue was the most horrendous part of the history at Ramle prison.

This Nitzan part of the prison was entirely underground, where for light only small dull light bulbs were used in each cell.

In daytime, a tiny window was blocked by a large iron bar.

Some prisoners would wait patiently for a tiny ray of afternoon sun to shine through and rest for a short time on their hands

Around the clock we would see and smell the rancid sewage leak from drains that were lying on the roofs of our cells.

In wintertime, in our cold, stinking hell many of the prisoners would get very sick. I remember once an outbreak of scabies, a highly contagious skin condition, where the main symptom is intense itching and it affected all the inmates.

During this time the administration would bring prisoners, even though their health was suffering, to the Nitzan Ramle prison for interrogation.

With all this agony and pain, we took a decision in 1992 to go on hunger strike in a bid among others, to have the 'section of rats' closed.

We won with our stomachs and frail bodies and had the chamber of horrors closed and solitary punishment lifted.

Prisoners came out of isolation; sick inmates left the underground hell of the Nitzan section and went back to regular prison life.

It is well known that the administration of the Israeli Prison Service does not abide by international humanitarian laws and does not respect worldwide rules, regarding the rights of prisoners. ∎

Zuhair Salah Al-Chechnya is a 54-year-old former Palestinian political prisoner. He spent twenty one years in Israeli jails and was released in October 2011 as part of the Shalit swap deal. He lives in the Gaza Strip.

A Bird in Prison

Mohammed Hassan
Palestine

WHILE on hunger strike in Israeli jails, I recalled how I took care of a bird and fed him in my cell, granting him freedom, which I needed the most.

Everything here is broken, the moving world outside is suspended between four walls, the clock moves only for the sake of moving.

Every minute feels like an hour and every hour feels like a day and days feel like years. All we have is a lifetime of memories in this prison.

This is how it felt during my time under administrative detention in Israeli occupation prisons.

Back then my mind often paused at the time when my children were young. For over twenty-four years I had only known the world of four walls, moving from prison to prison, cell to cell since I was sentenced to life.

Worrying about how my children had grown and how they were, consumed me night and day.

The pain of not knowing if they were healthy and happy broke my heart. I also longed for news of my wife and how she was coping.

I constantly searched for ways of sending greetings to them because in 1998 we had no means of communicating with our families.

In the prison open-air area, we were allowed a two-hour break around sunset.

I often looked up at the high fence, topped with barbed wire, where rays of the sun sometimes violated the authorities' wishes and pierced the overhead netting, reaching our skin.

One day I spotted a young bird falling from his parent's nest, which was on top of an electricity pole.

I rushed over and carried the tiny creature in my hand into my cell and into our small world.

I made him a home; a nest from cardboard and lined in with old newspapers. I placed the nest beside my bed to give him warmth in the harsh winter nights.

Day after day our new stranger became one of us and found the tenderness in me he would have received from his parents.

All my fellow inmates were astonished as our little friend

grew stronger. Every morning after I woke up, I would put his beak in my mouth and give him some water from my body. He would repay me by singing, to bring joy each day, before I'd feed him some old bread crumbs for his breakfast.

As I cleaned his little nest of paper he would then move from bed to bed, greeting each prisoner.

My little friend created a wonderful atmosphere and brought us birdsong and happiness to brighten our dark and dreary world.

On one occasion prison guards burst into our cell, they saw the little creature and tried to prevent me from holding him, his tiny body sprang from my trembling hand, he fluttered out of our cell, down a corridor and flew out an open prison window.

I told the jailer, "He will be back."

The jailer said to me, "Were you not ashamed of imprisoning a bird in here?"

I shouted, "He leaves and returns whenever he pleases, but you criminals, you hold thousands of people here."

An hour passed but it felt like years. I tortured myself that maybe I hadn't taken good care of the tiny bird or was it him who didn't have mercy on my weaknesses.

I reassured myself with the facts that I had fed him, cleaned his nest and provided him with all the comforts a man could give.

That evening, the silence in the cell was broken by the sound of tiny fluttering wings: he had returned.

My heart was filled with joy, I was so happy with his return.

Holding him in the palm of my hand I asked him, "Where were you and how is the world outside?"

He perched on my shoulder and started to sing before returning to his paper nest, his home beside my bed.

O God, I prayed, I wish I were a bird so as I could fly out of this prison. I wish this bird knew our language so as I could send him with messages to my family every morning and evening.

I told him he could leave any time and have his freedom, but he just put his head under one of his wings, as if to say he would never leave us.

I also told him, "My family lives in Al-Mughraqa, do you understand? You must find them and tell them of my longing."

It was a hard and emotionally difficult night for me.

As time went by the bird became more attached to everyone in the room.

There was a hunger strike while he was still there. We only had water, I was forced to open a window for him to fly out and find food for himself, as we had nothing to feed him or ourselves with, not even crumbs.

One day a new prisoner who didn't know about the bird came to our cell. I was having a shower and the bird was sleeping on my bed.

I returned to find the prisoner sitting on the bird, I hurried over and pushed him from the bed.

I cried out, "Move, move". but I was too late, the little bird was dead.

A part of my body died that night with the loss of the little creature, who was my only link with the outside world.

My inmates comforted me, but the sadness of his loss stayed with me for a long time. May God have mercy on us. Ever since I left the prison, thanks to the bird, I know the true meaning of freedom. ■

Mohammad Hassan was a former Palestinian political prisoner who died in September 2017 at the age of 60 from a chronic disease. He was married with 5 children, two of whom were killed in 2004 and 2012 by Israeli fire. He was released in October 2011 as part of the Shalit prisoner swap deal.

Snatching Human Rights with Stomachs and Blood

Mohammed Al-Dirawi
Palestine

I HAVE always been known by my nickname, Hamada, a name I got from when I was in prison. My full name is Mohammed Ibrahim Al-Dirawi. In 2011, I was released under the Shalit prisoner swap deal, after ten years in prison.

I am forty-two years old and married with two children.

The mass hunger strike of 2004 which lasted eighteen days, was the first hunger strike that I took part in, along with a large number of prisoners, mainly those arrested by the Israeli occupation forces during Al-Aqsa Intifada. They were mostly young people.

These youths filled the prisons after the rebellion.

The night before the strike began, as a mark of protest, we threw out all our food and electrical appliances, we only kept pillows, beds and some clothes.

Salt, the vital dietary requirement for any strike was in short supply, so what we had, we mixed with water in bottles and shared them among ourselves.

Following the beginning of the strike I began to feel dizzy and prayed, while sitting on my bed.

During the strike I couldn't sleep on my stomach, back or right-hand side.

My stomach started to bleed but I didn't want to show any pain, especially in front of a fellow prisoner Nael Al-Barghouthi, who had since a youth, spent thirty-seven years in prison.

Not revealing my agony, I would force my legs to walk to the toilet to relieve myself.

Nael said to me, "Hamada, if you cannot continue, you could break your strike."

At that stage, all of us had to decide if we would give up our lives if we didn't achieve our demands.

I know that every success since 2007: such as having access to electricity; TV or electronics, heating or cooling fans along with the supply of mattresses and the improvements in the quality of food, with more frequent family visits granted, was won by the hunger strike protests.

The 2002 and 2004 hunger strikes failed because the new young prisoners, although enthusiastic had little experience of what to expect on a hunger protest.

Also, the media didn't play any important role in the coverage of the strikes. Unfortunately, there were divisions among the factions within the prisons which didn't help.

A hunger strike remains the final weapon of the prisoners, although it is a tough and last resort in the battle to receive basic human rights inside Israeli prisons.

In those times the Israeli Prison Service (IPS) threatened the sick among us and those who suffered pain due to the strikes were prevented from receiving medication or painkillers, in a bid to pressure them to end their protests.

The hunger strikes for us were a torturous gamble with our lives.

Much of the treatment and abuse of the hunger strikers in Israeli occupation prisons blatantly violated human rights, rights all mankind are entitled to.

How is it legitimate to keep an ill prisoner between four walls, when he should be freed instead of being blackmailed to end his hunger strike in return for his health and life?

In reality what changes the prisoners' conditions and prevents the occupation from violating international laws and inmates' rights is the popular support from prisoners, governments and organisations worldwide, who support the Palestinian cause.

The Israeli occupation's crimes against Palestinians held in their jails are among the biggest crimes in the world.

Prisoners have no choice but to defend their human rights, with their stomachs, bodies and blood in the deadly gamble of a hunger strike. ■

Mohammed Al-Dirawi is a 43-year-old former Palestinian political prisoner who is married with two children. He is currently unemployed. He served eleven years of a 30-year sentence in the Israeli jails and was released in October 2011 as part of the Shalit prisoners swap deal and lives in the Gaza Strip.

Close to Death

Pat Sheehan
Ireland

I DON'T remember the exact date – just that it was a few weeks before Bobby Sands began his hunger strike, when I had a visit with my mother, father and my sister Louise.

My parents had been overjoyed when the hunger strike in 1980 had ended, after fifty-three days, without anyone having died. They believed, like many others, that the issues which led to the hunger strike would be resolved. Given the fact that I had volunteered for that hunger strike and had joined it for the five days before it ended, it should not come as a surprise that my family were happy it was over.

Unfortunately, the issues were not resolved, and in the prison, we decided that another hunger strike was the only way to break the impasse. I volunteered again and, in fact, went a bit further by approaching Bobby Sands to ensure I was a part of it. He said he would speak to Bik McFarlane (the officer commanding IRA prisoners). I believed my name would be high up on the list.

The visit with my parents and sister was enjoyable and uneventful. We talked about family, the situation on the outside and, of course, the forthcoming hunger strike. They were aware I had volunteered yet the visit seemed relaxed with no attempts to persuade me to change my mind. It was also around the time of Louise's birthday. She would have turned twenty-four that month, a teacher of French and Physical Education, and was just over a year older than me.

When the visit ended, we all stood up. I kissed my mother and sister and shook hands with my father. He gripped my hand and stood his ground as my mother and sister moved towards the exit of the visiting room.

"I want you to take your name off the list of volunteers for the hunger strike," he said. "Louise has been diagnosed with leukaemia and given five or six years to live."

I was stunned. Speechless. However, there was no time for discussion anyway as the guards were already moving in to see why there was a delay in my father leaving.

When I returned to my cell, my head was spinning. I was devastated at having received such bad news but realised I now needed to consider what I was going to do. The first decision I made was not to tell any of my comrades in the prison about my sister's diagnosis. I rationalised that decision in my own mind in terms of not wanting anyone to think I was using Louise's illness to prepare the ground for withdrawing my name.

On reflection, however, I now understand that I had already made up my mind and was never going to change it.

To contemplate going on hunger strike I knew I had to focus entirely on what I needed to do. In a sense, my task was straightforward; I had to stay on hunger strike until the British government acceded to our demands or, failing that, until I was dead. In order to do that I needed to clear my mind of any distractions. For example, the media regularly reported that a possible breakthrough to resolve the hunger strike was close. Many of those stories came directly from the British and were aimed at building hope among the prisoners and their families and then dashing that hope. I had resolved not to allow rumours or speculation to have any impact. I would be satisfied that the hunger strike was over when Bik McFarlane informed me in person.

Likewise, I could not allow bad news, such as other hunger strikers dying, to deflect me from the course of action on which I intended to embark. It was with that mindset I faced into the prospect of fasting until death. I realised later that that is how I dealt with the terrible news about my sister's condition. I had erected a psychological defence that was impenetrable.

As my comrades died, I prepared myself for the day I would be called on. However, no word came and I was beginning to wonder why, so I eventually decided to write to Bik and ask what was happening. He wrote back and said that because of my sister's illness some people were suggesting that I might not be in the right frame of mind to go on hunger strike. I wrote back immediately and told him that my sister's condition had no bearing whatsoever on my decision or determination to go on hunger strike.

Pat Sheehan with the family of Palestinian hunger striker Samer Al-Issawi.

Within days, I received a written communication from the leadership to inform me that I had been selected to replace Kieran Doherty who had died on 2 August. The author of the communication asked me to reflect on my decision to embark on hunger strike and that if I had any doubts I should step aside and nothing less would be thought of me. However, it also stated that if I decided to go through with this course of action that I would be dead within two months.

How could I not have doubts when confronted with such stark finality and facing into the prospect of my own death at twenty-three-years of age? Nevertheless, I was as sure as I could be in my own mind that I could do what was required of me, and I took confidence from the fact that other comrades had already sacrificed their lives. If they could do it, then so could I. I wrote back to the leadership to tell them I was ready and that I would not let anyone down. I joined the hunger strike on 10 August, 1981. On 20 August Micky Devine became the tenth hunger striker to die in the prison hospital.

On my fifty-second day without food a consultant from one of the main hospitals in Belfast came into the prison and examined me. By this stage I weighed around 42kgs, I was almost blind, my body was yellow with jaundice and I was constantly vomiting green bile. I could no longer keep water down. The doctor told me that I was very seriously ill. He said my liver was enlarged and beginning to shut down and that even if I ended my hunger strike there and then he could not be sure that I would survive.

Three days later, at 3pm on 3 October, the decision was taken by the leadership to end the hunger strike. I was the volunteer longest on the strike at that time and therefore the person most likely to die next. Without doubt I had only a few days left to live.

Ten Irish republicans died on hunger strike between 5 May and 20 August, 1981: Bobby Sands, Francis Hughes, Raymond McCreesh, Patsy O'Hara, Joe McDonnell, Martin Hurson, Tom McElwee, Kevin Lynch, Kieran

Doherty, Micky Devine. It was, and remains, one of the most defining and momentous periods in Irish history.

My sister, Louise, died from leukaemia on 8 May, 1986, nine months before I was released from the H-Blocks, Long Kesh.

I believe if Louise had not been ill that I would have died in the H-Blocks on the hunger strike in 1981. ■

At the age of fifteen, Pat Sheehan survived an attempt by loyalist gunmen to kill him. He served nine years in the H-Blocks and was out of prison just two years when he was again arrested and charged with having a booby-trapped bomb and sentenced to twenty-four years. He served another nine years and was released under the terms of the Good Friday Agreement and was subsequently elected to the Northern Ireland Assembly for Sinn Féin. He is head of Sinn Féin's Middle-East desk and has visited Palestine many times.

Seven Hunger Strikes

Jehad Abughabin
Palestine

I AM Jehad Abughabin, I spent twenty-three and a half years in Israeli occupation prisons.

When I first entered jail, my hair was black, it turned grey and later white. Before I was released in the 2011 Shalit prisoner swap deal, I had taken part in seven different hunger strikes.

For me at forty-eight, I believe prison is a huge experience, full of bitterness along with suffering and it's a struggle that's difficult to describe.

I spent most of my young life in a prison cell, three metres wide by seven metres long, which usually held at least fourteen men.

I felt misery in that jail, especially when we were attacked by prison guards using gas or pepper sprays, causing us severe pain as our eyes burned.

Only the International Committee of the Red Cross (ICRC) got permits from the Israeli occupation to visit us. Other human rights bodies were unaware of what was happening in the jail.

Access to inmates by the ICRC was only granted at times chosen by the prison authorities which allowed them time to hide evidence of their cruelty.

The Red Cross could see our suffering, they always listened to the prisoners and noted their concerns.

They gained access to us through a heavy steel door and visited us in our dark rooms, which only had small windows. Sunlight seldom crept into our cells or our lives. Through the years, I found that on hunger strike you become very thin, after just a week you constantly feel dizzy and are barely able to speak. It becomes impossible to stand without falling.

The last strike I took part in was in August 2008 when my stomach declined to accept water on the second day.

Every time I drank, I would vomit, but I had no choice but to try and try again, hoping to force my stomach to keep the water with salt down.

I was successful, continued my strike and was not forced to quit in humiliation, which would have pleased the prison authorities and the Shin Beth security service. In my forties and fifties, after many years in captivity and multiple experiences of hunger protests, my body became less able to cope with the strikes.

On the fifth day of my last hunger strike, prison officers burst into my cell and took me to solitary, where I started talking to myself.

I was alone in a cell, fighting its walls and passing the time just breathing the thin air. All I had was a little water and salt.

During a strike one faces many challenges, the most important is how to maintain your health, so that you don't have to go to the medical clinic, which in fact can be a torture chamber in an Israeli prison.

There, we were promised painkillers if we agreed to end our strike, but only received paracetamol.

There were great successes in the general strike of 1992, when the Palestinian people in the West Bank and Gaza rose in solidarity with the prisoners. They stood together behind the strike and provided popular support for it.

I was in Nafha prison, we were on the nineteenth day, only because we started our strike five days before the others.

Seventeen Palestinians were martyred and more than 1,000 people were captured by the occupation authorities.

Rabin, Israel's Prime Minister then, was forced to send his Minister of Police, Moshe Shahil, to negotiate with the prisoners.

On the fourteenth day of the strike, a committee of the prisoners, led by Qadura Faris, the then prisoners' leader negotiated with him.

Faris, along with Brother Jabr Wishah, one of the veteran leaders of the prisoners and with inmate Maher Abulouf, spoke to him on our behalf.

The Minister of Police, Shahil, sent a special committee, led by the retired director of Israeli prisons Shaul Levy along with a Shabak officer from Rabin's office, known as Abu Ghazal, who was responsible for investigations in Gaza during the 1980s. They agreed that prisoners would end their strike in return for family visits from the 1 December, two months after the strike.

They also allowed cooking equipment in prison, and gave permission for prisoners to have photographs taken with their children, wives, parents and relatives.

A demand for regular supply of clothes and books, requested by prisoners was also granted.

Achieving success in the strike was difficult for the prisoners and it was greatly assisted by the external support of campaigners that forced the prison authorities to meet our humanitarian demands. ■

Jehad Abughabin is a 50-year-old former Palestinian political prisoner who is married with three children. He is working for the Palestinian National Security and has spent twenty three years in Israeli jails. He was released in October 2011 as part of the Shalit prisoners swap deal and lives in the Gaza Strip.

Demonstrators protesting in solidarity with Palestinian hunger strikers wearing blind folds to highlight the experience of Palestinian prisoners in Israeli jails.

I was Eighteen During My First Hunger Strike

Tarik Al-Modallal
Palestine

I WAS arrested when I was fourteen on 19 January, 2000 and released on 12 January, 2018. I spent nearly eighteen years in jail. I married two months after my release.

In prison I was the representative of the Palestinian Islamic Jihad movement for the Karama (dignity) hunger strike which began on 17 April, 2017, and lasted forty-two days.

I experienced three collective strikes: the general strike of 2004, the 2000 strike and the general strike of 2017. I was only eighteen during the general strike of 2004.

I was representative of the Islamic Jihad movement in Nafha prison, when Fatah called for a strike, but Hamas refused.

The prison administration waited for Islamic Jihad to announce its position but I didn't tell them until the last minute.

On the morning of the strike the prison guards took me to the Ramleh isolation torture section, which was used to break the prisoners' will.

An officer tried to convince me not to join the strike saying, "Retract your deal with Fatah. We promise that the prisoners of Islamic Jihad will not be searched in prisons. We will give you a section of your own and improve the quality of your food." I replied, "You are too late. If you want anything, talk to the strike committee, they are the only group authorised to discuss the strike."

The committee set out their grievances:

1. The first reason for the strike was to stop the harassment of female prisoners by putting them in with common criminal Israeli prisoners.
2. The second issue was the lack of medical care for sick prisoners and the failure to provide treatment for them, other than sending ill inmates to the Ramleh prison repeatedly, without their medical needs addressed.
3. To prevent attacks on prisoners by Israeli units armed with dogs, while the prison guards look on without taking any action.
4. To halt the arbitrary transfer of inmates from prisons

and sections by the Nashon Unit where prisoners in transit were abused, humiliated, searched and starved while ill prisoners are medically neglected.

5. To change the practice of inmates' visiting families being harassed and not allowed to take anything in to the prisoners, also to alter the practice of visits being reduced to one every two months and to end the prevention of visits of families from Gaza.

6. The demand to set up phone lines to allow inmates to contact their families, with a specific minimum call time allowed for each prisoner.

In addition, the hunger strikers highlighted the absence of meat, eggs and vegetables in the canteen.

The hunger strikers' demands were fundamental, and concerned rights, guaranteed by international law but the Israeli occupation does not abide by international laws.

The strike was broken at Jaloba prison on the fourth day in exchange for minor improvements.

Out of 2,000 striking prisoners, 800 remained on hunger strike, half of them in Nafha prison and the remaining half in the rest of the prisons.

The main reason for the failure of the 2017 protest was that the negotiations were not held with the National Committee of the strike. The success of any strike is that no negotiations should take place without the involvement of the National Committee. The prison leaders often refused to implement the concessions agreed with the strikers' leaders.

The last word should have been with the National Committee, but that didn't happen, as the prison authorities managed to convince the prisoners' leaders in jails like Asqalan and Ramle and others to end their hunger strikes.

Disputes took place among Fatah prisoners which also weakened the strike.

This hunger strike campaign was the hardest I have experienced, it lasted forty-two days, some inmates lost their hearing and sight.

Many hunger strikers suffered kidney problems, including two who experienced kidney failure.

All were affected by problems with their digestive systems.

The key to the success of any hunger strike is the discipline of the prisoners, old veterans and new-comers should follow what the Supreme Committee of the strike declares.

The Committee is usually strategically isolated by the prison authorities. However, there is always an alternative leadership ready to step in to represent the prisoners and make demands on their behalf. ■

Tarik Al-Modallal is a 35-year-old former Palestinian political prisoner who spent fourteen years in Israeli jails. He was released in January 2018 after serving his sentence and lives in Rafah city in the Gaza Strip.

Too Much Sugar Following a Hunger Strike

Ali Almughrabi
Palestine

MY name is Ali Yousef Almughrabi, I'm from Al-Dheisheh refugee camp in Bethlehem in the West Bank. I was arrested on 25 July on charges of killing a number of settlers and Israeli occupation soldiers. I was given two life sentences, in addition to thirty-two years in jail.

I was a member of a resistance cell which included my brother Mahmud who was martyred in 2000, and my brother Ahmed, currently in detention after he was given eighteen life sentences and fifty years.

I spent nine and a half years in prison and was released in the 2011 Shalit prisoner swap deal. Hunger strikes in Israeli occupation prisons are either individual or collective protests.

I participated in my first collective hunger strike in 2004, before that I was part of an independent strike in support of child prisoners.

The complex feelings of a hunger striker cannot be measured, because it is so wide, deep, also personal and taking part in that form of protest is a difficult decision.

As in 2004, all actions in a protest needed to be agreed with all factions, through the National Committee dealing with hunger strikes.

The protest back then was planned and coordinated for two years in advance and included all prisons.

The Supreme Committee decided on the demands of prisoners, according to their priorities and set the hour for the launch of the strike.

When a protest begins, a committee is authorised to negotiate with the Israeli Prison Service (IPS) on behalf of the prisoners.

Before a strike, a committee, called 'the operations room' is formed.

Its task is to protect the striking prisoners and maintain discipline.

Participating prisoners are advised about the pre-strikes and strike periods and updates are sent to all prisoners.

They are instructed how to control the movements of their weak bodies in their cells and reminded that they are not to read, walk or talk.

Prisoners are told that under no circumstances are they to speak to the IPS.

One of our demands back then, considered a basic human right, was to have all prisoners removed from solitary confinement.

Among the inmates were my brothers: Ahmad Almughrabi; Hassan Salama and Mahmoud Issa.

Another demand was that family visits should not be done through a glass barrier but through nets, which would allow prisoners better access to their loved ones.

The barriers prevented prisoners from hugging their children and embracing their wives, mothers and relatives.

Telephone landlines are permitted in prisons throughout the world, we demanded access to phones, so that we could speak to our families.

We also insisted on improvements in the quality and quantity of prison food.

All of our demands were in keeping with the basic rights, guaranteed by international law.

The experience of going on hunger strike is very harsh and goes against human instincts.

Man eats, drinks and sleeps in peace and we protested against not being allowed these human necessities.

We resisted the prison authorities but at the same time we hurt ourselves, but not the enemy holding us in captivity.

The experience of the 2004 strike was difficult for me. I couldn't imagine sitting for eighteen days and not eating.

Strikes are physically exhausting on the body and it feels like knives piercing your stomach, because your body needs food along with vitamins and we deprived ourselves of getting them.

The time spent during the first three days getting used to the new abnormal situation passes calmly.

One of the most painful problems is that our bodies do not accept salt with water, there are inmates who can't tolerate it and would vomit. These victims would lose their ability to walk or move, by the seventh or eighth day.

I was exhausted and felt physically and mentally drained as never before.

To this day, I still suffer from my time on hunger strike.

During the protest, I tried to occupy myself with prayers.

I couldn't sleep, my agony felt like torture and I wasn't allowed painkillers.

By the eighteenth day of that strike I had lost twelve kilos, every day the prison administration weighed us.

Our bodies, due to the serious lack of food in the hunger strike gave off an unpleasant odour.

When we ended the strike I didn't comply with the instructions of the National Committee to suspend the action and suspension is different from ending the strike totally.

The suspension might last a half day or maybe two or three hours.

During the suspension, the prison administration gives us breaks in the sun and allowed us to have fruit juices.

Soon we began to share biscuits, sugar and juice.

In a reckless moment, hunger drove me to eat seven spoons of sugar at once.

A fellow prisoner was angry and warned me about the danger on a hunger striker's body from a sudden intake of so much sugar.

I told him, "I couldn't concentrate and didn't have enough patience to mix it with water."

The next day, I was in severe pain, suffering from cramps and constipation, I was unable to attend Friday prayers.

Despite the failure of the strike to achieve strategic objectives, some tactical matters, such as food, where a kilo and a half of meat and the same weight in vegetables, a month, were allowed in the prison.

Much to our disappointment, prisoners were to remain in solitary confinement and the glass barriers were to remain between us and our families during visits.

The truth is that this was very difficult for us to take.

Looking back now, we learned lessons from that strike and were it not for the hunger protests, conditions for the prisoners would not have improved.

In the history of our successful hunger strikes: the first was aimed at not having to address a jailer as 'Sir' when we were being counted.

The second was to be given better mattresses to sleep on and the third was to get access to paper and pens.

In order to be allowed listen to a radio or have electric fans in their cells, prisoners had no options but to strike again.

The supply of more and better-quality food in prison canteens was yet another milestone, won by sacrifices made by the sick and wounded inmates along with the martyrs, who gave their lives in protests

A hunger strike is a bitter experience and passive resistance, it means hurting ourselves so as to send a forceful message to our oppressors and the outside world. ∎

Ali Almughrabi is a former Palestinian political prisoner who was released in October 2011 as part of the Shalit swap deal. He lives in the Gaza strip after being deported from Bethlehem in the West Bank.

Five Demands

Tommy McKearney
Ireland

IRELAND has long experience of political turmoil arising from resistance to the mistreatment of its people by British colonialism and its fellow travellers. The determination of Irish people to break free from their oppressor erupted into armed insurrection on many occasions. Many fighting men died while others were imprisoned but resistance continued. Even when imprisoned, Irish patriots remained unbroken and unbreakable. Below is my personal reflection on events in this cycle in which I had a small part while imprisoned.

Well before the most recent Irish insurrection, imprisoned Irish freedom fighters refused to compromise or conform to their jailers' dictates. In the mid-19th century, the legendary Fenian Jeremiah O'Donovan Rossa rebelled against Britain's prison system. The 1920s witnessed a constant struggle between republican prisoners and their captors. Most notable was the death on hunger strike of iconic figures such as Thomas Ashe and Lord Mayor of Cork City, Terence Mac Swiney. Indeed, such was the impact of Terence Mac Swiney's heroic struggle that his passing was globally newsworthy. A youthful Ho Chi Minh wrote of the Irish patriot's death while revolutionaries in China and India also drew inspiration from his sacrifice.

Reared within this tradition, my generation of Irish republican freedom fighters also rebelled against intolerable prison conditions. Veteran IRA member Billy McKee led a hunger strike in 1972, forcing the British to concede 'special category status'. And when, three years later, British authorities sought to resile from this arrangement, republican prisoners again refused to acquiesce.

As part of this attempt to undermine the integrity of the Irish struggle, British authorities launched a campaign to discredit captured members of the Irish Republican Army by denying them recognition as captured combatants. The British attempted to portray Irish Republican resistance, not as a battle for national liberation but as a tawdry criminal enterprise.

In an effort to illustrate this deceptive narrative, Britain's jailers sought to degrade imprisoned freedom fighters by dressing them in the garb of common criminals. When Irish republican prisoners refused to wear this shameful uniform, they were stripped naked, confined to cell and frequently beaten. Deprived of their own clothing and refusing to wear prison criminal uniform, republican prisoners resorted to wrapping themselves in prison blankets and hence the sobriquet, 'Blanket Men'.

In spite of being routinely mistreated within a brutal prison regime, republican prisoners retained an amazing resilience, demonstrating an incredible degree of fortitude. Their remarkable spirit proved an inspiration for their friends, relatives and supporters at home and abroad. The republican cause gained increasing support from other progressive elements in Ireland and anti-imperialist communities abroad.

Those hostile to the notion of Irish independence grew increasingly concerned. The idea that Ireland, such a small country, could force the British to leave its shores was a prospect that worried imperialists everywhere. This, after all, was a time when a New World Order was being planned and implemented by the United States and Britain. In this context, breaking the prison protest was seen as a vital step in defeating the battle for Irish liberation.

Certain factors in particular caused the politically-motivated propaganda assault to assume a new and critical stage in 1979 when Margaret Thatcher became Prime Minister of the United Kingdom, a few short months after Karol Wojtyła was elevated to the papacy as Pope John Paul II.

When in September of 1979 Pope John Paul II visited the Republic of Ireland (but not the North) he virtually endorsed Britain's stance vis-à-vis Ireland and denounced the IRA. He said 'murder is murder'. But it was selective and was directed against criminalising Irish republicanism and its proud anti-imperialist history. It gave an enormous propaganda advantage to Margaret Thatcher who frequently quoted his words. Her confidence was soon to be further buoyed by the rising popularity in the United States of the reactionary Ronald Reagan.

As on other occasions, the British government's calculation had much to do with domestic politics. Margaret Thatcher and her Tory party were elected, determined to implement what we now recognise as the initial stage of a global drive to install ruthless, right-wing neoliberalism. This involved (and continues to do so) transferring wealth to the already well-off by a brutal process of union-busting, industrial closures and diminishing the welfare safety net. Thatcher and her ministers saw the conflict with Irish republican prisoners as an opportunity to demonstrate to an English public their resolute firmness, regardless of what the consequences might be for Ireland. Consequences that were to be manifold, complex and long-lasting.

With a new and ultra-right-wing imperialist in 10 Downing Street enjoying the support of the Vatican and the US for its Irish policies, republican prisoners were forced to begin a process of deep analysis and reflection that ultimately led to hunger strike.

While the immediate rationale for this drastic option was dire prison conditions, a greater issue was at stake. The British policy of 'criminalisation' of republican prisoners' was intent on undermining the Irish independence struggle. Imprisoned Irish republicans knew they could not afford to concede ground in the struggle for recognition of their status as political prisoners. To do otherwise their cause would suffer.

By coincidence, the transfer of several senior IRA personnel, including Bobby Sands, Brendan Hughes and Brendan McFarlane, to the wing in which I was held led to my direct involvement in the events that followed. While not a member of that senior leadership, I was asked to reflect quietly on different strategic options. In reality, room for manoeuvre was growing less as time went by and eventually, I came to share the view held by the prisoners' commander, Brendan Hughes, that we had no alternative but to plan for a hunger strike. From my conversations with Brendan Hughes (and his close confidant Bobby Sands), I know that this was a decision they took with considerable reluctance, albeit with absolute conviction.

However, the IRA leadership, that is, those at liberty and in overall control of the organisation, hesitated about authorising such a decisive step. For a number of months, a secret dialogue continued between prisoners' leaders and the IRA high command. Both understood the importance of the issue. Prisoners were fearful of losing out over a protracted struggle while the high command was conscious of the cost involved in losing in a head-to-head conflict with a brutal British government.

Nevertheless, towards the end of 1980, the IRA high command gave its consent for a hunger strike. To a certain extent, this was a relief for those of us involved in the considerations. The die was now cast.

While those embarking on a hunger strike must be prepared to die, it is not a suicide pact but rather it is a desperate struggle to achieve an acceptable settlement for matters that cannot otherwise be resolved. Therefore, and although the decision was taken in principle to proceed, it was important to decide how to engage tactically and strategically.

First, there was a need to identify the precise demand that had to be registered. Prior to this there had been a generalised call to restore political status. In consultation with comrades outside the prison, it was decided to define the issue more clearly and make a list of five demands. These were to be: 1) the right to wear own clothing; 2) right not to carry out prison work; 3) right to freedom of association; 4) restoration of lost remission; 5) right to receive a weekly food parcel.

Contrary to some misleading reports, the prisoner leadership was always willing to adopt a pragmatic and realistic position. It was recognised from the outset that the primary objective of the hunger strike was to achieve a tolerable beachhead from which to advance. With their history, the IRA prisoners knew that improving conditions was often an incremental process over many months if not indeed years. In this context it was understood that it would be possible to allow a certain degree of flexibility around the interpretation of some of the five demands.

While aware of the wider ramifications and considerations of the decision, the situation had become very personal for me. I was to be one of seven men, from across the Six-Counties, chosen to take part in what was to be the 1980 hunger strike. With my participation confirmed, there was the difficult task of informing my family of my decision.

This is an aspect of that period sometimes overlooked. It is agonising and difficult at any time to watch a close relative slowly approach death. Almost always this end-of-life process is the unavoidable consequence of ill-health, disease, or old age. The slow death on hunger strike of a healthy young adult is something entirely different as relatives and friends struggled desperately to offer moral support to their loved one while endeavouring to persuade those in power to change their position and allow the conflict to end without loss of life.

My hunger strike ended after fifty-three days in controversial circumstances. Although nothing had been committed to paper, it appeared clear to the IRA prisoners' leader Brendan Hughes that as a result of several overtures, the British authorities were willing to affect an acceptable compromise. His dilemma was that in terms of realpolitik this had to take place before one of his men died. He understood British government thinking on this issue. London would see, he realised, the inevitable response to the death of a republican hunger striker as conceding significant publicity and political credibility to the IRA. Britain would not further enhance an IRA publicity coup (as they would interpret it) by thereafter also granting the prisoners' demands.

When the British failed to either honour their unspoken assurances or even to avail of a window of opportunity to settle the issue constructively, they ensured that there would be another hunger strike and on this occasion with prisoners now and understandably refusing to accept verbal assurances or promises, ten men died.

With the advantage of hindsight and the passing of four decades, it is possible to reflect analytically on the events of that period.

To begin with it is necessary to highlight several crucial factors. In the first instance, the British government held an enormous advantage having the ability to exercise state power over prison conditions and also wielded great influence over the media as well. Moreover, the British government could have created the conditions that would have ended the hunger strikes at any stage had it wished to do so.

When the final hunger strike ended in late 1981, it occurred without the British government having made concessions to the prisoners. Margaret Thatcher, her Tory party and its supporters and the right-wing media in Britain and Ireland hailed this outcome as a triumph for resolute government and a defeat for Irish republicanism. The reality was not just different but much more complex.

Contrary to the Thatcher narrative, jailed republicans had by any reasonable reckoning achieved recognition as political prisoners. With tens of thousands of supporters on the streets across Ireland and significant backing in the USA and Europe, coupled with the election of several hunger strikers, including the iconic Bobby Sands to Westminster, they had won this objective by popular acclamation in the eyes of the world. Years later, during the Good Friday Agreement negotiations, crafty British civil service was to tacitly recognise this reality by introducing the concept of 'politically motivated' prisoners.

Moreover, such was the unmanageable turmoil generated in Ireland, coupled with international interest in the Irish situation at the time that the British authorities felt compelled to give ground. In the days following the end of the hunger strike a British cabinet minister announced that his government would grant all prisoners in Northern Irish jails the right to wear their own clothes, allow a weekly food parcel and arranged for the restoration of much of forfeited remission. Apart from begging the question why this had not happened earlier, it meant that not only did London concede a significant chunk of the five demands but by doing so, effectively acknowledged the merit of the prisoners' struggle.

Within a few years, the issue of work was also resolved when the authorities decided that in the interest of 'prison security' it was best not to have republicans in the workshops or gardens. Indeed, by the mid-1980s it would have been difficult for the uninitiated to discern the difference between the then existing prison regime and what republicans had been asking for in early 1980.

In the wider context the 'Year of Hunger Strike' had a profound impact on the political situation in Ireland. Irish republicanism had demonstrated that it enjoyed huge support and was a political force to be reckoned with. Simultaneously, it dispelled the claim that it was the ideology of a 'fanatical few, holding communities to ransom by threat of force'. Moreover, the emergence of a republican mass movement led to the eventual displacement of the middle-class SDLP as the voice of non-unionists in the Six Counties. Republicans have argued, and continue to do, over whether best advantage has been taken from this development but it is indisputable that the nationalist working class was no longer patronised and misrepresented by self-serving Catholic placemen.

In conclusion, allow me attempt to answer two questions. One relates to the viability, under contemporary conditions, of hunger strike as an option of struggle for the oppressed. The second question is more specific to the Irish events of four decades past – was it worth the price paid?

There is no simple answer to the first question. What has to be kept in mind is that government agencies the world over have studied the Irish hunger strikes and consequently have been working on their response. Some have devised effective force-feeding techniques. Others have planned for intensive propaganda counter-offensives. Elsewhere, authoritarian regimes are simply prepared to be indifferent. Ultimately, it is a very personal decision for the individual or individuals involved and then only as a last resort.

To the second question, it may well be necessary to echo Zhou Enlai and suggest that it's still too early to assess the full import of those events. Nevertheless, there is undoubtedly truth in the old adage that to fight is to risk losing but to refuse to fight is to guarantee failure. What we can say with absolute certainty is that in Ireland, those who have given their lives on hunger strike retain a special place in the people's affection and memory and without doubt, their sacrifice has helped change history. ■

Tommy McKearney is a socialist republican and former IRA member who spent fifty-three days on hunger strike while imprisoned for sixteen years by the British. During the course of the 25-year struggle he had three brothers and an uncle killed. Sean was killed on IRA active service; Padraig was also killed on active service when he and seven other IRA Volunteers were shot by the SAS; and Kevin and his Uncle John were assassinated by pro-British loyalists.

Tommy is the author of The Provisional IRA, from insurrection to parliament *and joint author of* Between Sectarianism and Neo-Liberalism: The State of Northern Ireland and the Democratic Deficit. *He writes a regular column for the monthly* Socialist Voice.

Originally from County Tyrone, he now lives south of the border in Monaghan.

A Daughter's Prayer for her Captive Father

Khalil Abu Aram

*I yearn for you whenever a dawn breaks
or a night passes without seeing you.*

*Every day my yearning, and grief, increase for you
and I pass another night in your memory.*

*How sorry I feel that even grief becomes weary
for your presence, your care, your protection.*

*Even when my longing for you becomes unbearable,
I find myself growing old without you.*

*The dregs of infancy I sip with bitterness,
and the sorrow for my lost youth will be felt when I meet you.*

*I lay out my uniform, my bag –
perhaps one day I can trace your gentle steps to school.*

*I look around me left and right
but do not see anything, save dreams of a memory.*

Though my cheeks are worn down with tears,
a fire, I light in my soul for you.

I swear, by God, and the pain of my youth,
your absence guides me.

Age has driven away childhood
but my heart still beats to your steps.

I am innocent and my name is Ameera,
so how can your princess, in all her innocence, forget you.

© Issam Rimawi

Palestinian women hold photos of Bilal Kayid and Mahmoud Albalboul held by Israel under administrative detention without a charge or trial.

Acknowledgements

"OUR chains will be broken before we are, because it is human nature to heed the call for freedom regardless of the cost." Marwan Barghouti, Palestinian political prisoner, hunger striker and party leader.

Not many of us are willing to make that ultimate sacrifice for freedom, and perhaps can't come close to understanding people who do. By publishing this book, we wanted to give the readers access to the thoughts and feelings of Palestinian and Irish hunger strikers who were ready for this ultimate sacrifice.

We would like to thank journalists Moath Alamoudi and Fayhaa Shalash for conducting the interviews with the Palestinian (former) hunger-strikers in Gaza and the West Bank, respectively. The majority of the interviewees are in Gaza, many having been deported from their homes in the West Bank. Fayhaa's interviewees included her own husband Muhammad Al-Qeeq who endured 94 days on a hunger strike to protest his administrative detention. Our thanks also goes to Issam Rimawi who kindly provided many of the photographs used in this book.

We would like to express our gratitude to Prof Richard Falk for writing the Foreword, and reminding us always that civil society needs to step up where governments have failed, in order to achieve justice for the Palestinians.

Much appreciation for the work of Dr. Asad Abu Sharkh who wrote the Introduction to this book and edited the text. Many thanks also to Tom Ryan and Michael Cuddy, for proofreading the text and improving its quality.

Dr. Asad also connected us to Danny Morrison, a prolific writer and activist for the Irish Republican cause, who got us the narratives of the Irish hunger strikers, and who facilitated publication through An Fhuiseog, Falls Road, Belfast. We would also like to mention Sinn Féin International Department, the Bobby Sands Trust and EuroPal for their valuable assistance.

Like flowers growing through a crack in the concrete, Palestinian poetry flourishes in Israeli prisons, and we are immensely grateful to Naveed Ashraf for giving us access to the poems of Palestinian prisoner and hunger-striker Khalil Abu Aram which he painstakingly translated. We also wish to thank Hajra Bibi Islam and Talha Ahsan, for their help and advice in editing these translations.

Last but not least, heartfelt thanks to Low Seong Chai our book designer for *The Prisoners' Diaries: Palestinian Voices from the Israeli Gulag* and *Dreaming of Freedom: Palestinian Child Prisoners Speak* who, once again, has enabled us to deliver the words of those behind bars to the world outside.

Without the collective efforts of those mentioned above and many others who have unfailingly supported the work we do , these stories would not have seen the light of day.

We are very much indebted for all your contributions and we hope that these stories reach many people across the globe. May God bless each and everyone of you.

Norma Hashim & Yousef M. Aljamal
May 2021

A timeline of Palestinian mass hunger strikes in Israel

Ramle Prison: 11 Days
Palestinian political prisoners protest against meagre portions and poor-quality food, as well as the policy of banning writing stationery and being forced to address their jailers as "sir". The strike ends when prison authorities put the prisoners in solitary confinement, which has been classified as torture by several international human rights treaties.

Kfar Yona Prison: 8 Days
In conjunction with Ramle prison, Palestinian prisoners in the Kfar Yona prison protest similar conditions and also call on the Israeli prison authorities to replace their plastic sleeping mattresses. They were able to get the prison authorities to permit stationery for writing letters to their families.

Neve Tirza Women's Prison: 8 Days
Female prisoners call for improved prison conditions; they manage to improve ventilation, increase time in the prison yard, and allow in sanitary products from the Red Cross. During the hunger strike, prison authorities place fasting prisoners in solitary confinement as punishment.

Asqalan Prison: 7 Days

During this hunger strike in 1970, Abdul Qader Abu al-Fahm becomes the first Palestinian prisoner to die during a hunger strike. Al-Fahm dies as a result of force-feeding by Israeli prison authorities, who inserted a nasal feeding tube into his lungs instead of his stomach. Prisoners called for allowing stationery and clothes from their families, as well as increasing break time in the prison yard, but their requests were not fulfilled.

Asqalan Prison: 45 Days

Prisoners call for a general improvement of conditions inside the prisons. The prison administration allows entry of stationery, improves the quality and quantity of food and replaces plastic sleeping mattresses, but later revokes the changes.

Nafha Prison: 32 Days

Nafha prison, in the southern desert area, is one of the worst Israeli prisons; prisoners report being crammed into small, dirty cells that lack air conditioning with only small ventilation openings and receiving rotten food. Rasem Halawah and Ali Jafari die as a result of force-feeding during the hunger strike in 1980. Prison conditions are improved as a result of the strike.

Juneid Prison: 13 Days

Considered a turning point in the history of hunger strikes. Eight hundred prisoners reportedly join the strike for better conditions in the Nablus prison. Prisoners are crammed into overcrowded cells, suffer from a lack of ventilation and no reading material. The strike brought about many changes, such as bringing in a radio, TV, clothes and better-quality food.

Multiple Prisons: 20 Days
David Maimon is appointed head of the Israeli Prison Service and reverses many of the achievements of the previous strike. More than 3,000 prisoners participate, but the strike ends without any real achievements. It plays a part in the outbreak of the first Palestinian Intifada, or mass uprising.

Most Prisons: 19 Days
Considered one of the most successful hunger strikes in Palestinian history. Seven thousand prisoners stage the strike after the Labour Party wins the elections and amid speculations of negotiations between Israel and the Palestine Liberation Organization (PLO). The strike results in major achievements, such as shutting down the isolation section of Ramle prison, stopping strip searches, increasing family visitation time and allowing cooking slates into the cells.

Multiple Prisons: 29 Days
Launched after 80 prisoners in Hadarim prison are put in solitary confinement. At least 650 participate in the hunger strike, calling on prison authorities to allow telephone calls, a stop to strip searches and to release those in isolation.

They also protest against Israel's policy of forcing prisoners to see their families from behind glass barriers instead of nets. Some demands were met, but prison conditions worsened again with the start of the second Intifada.

Multiple Prisons: 18 Days

About 4,000 prisoners protest mainly against Israel's occupation of the Palestinian territories and demand improvements such as access to telephones, stopping strip searches, and removal of glass partitions during family visits. Prison authorities respond by removing books, newspapers, cigarettes and salt from the prisons to punish prisoners, as well as stopping family visits. The hunger strike fails to restore their rights, with the prison service not making any changes.

Multiple Prisons: 22 Days

Prisoners from the Popular Front for the Liberation of Palestine (PFLP) faction call on Israel to stop its use of solitary confinement and to release Ahmad Saadat, general secretary of the party, from isolation. Other demands were that Israel stop its policy of denying books and newspapers to prisoners and that it no longer keep prisoners shackled during family visits.

Multiple Prisons: 28 Days

On Palestinian Prisoners Day, approximately 2,000 prisoners participate in a hunger strike, demanding an end to administrative detention, as well as other punitive measures, such as isolation and denial of family visits. The prisoners end their strike after agreeing to a deal with Israel, mediated by Egypt and the Palestinian Authority, for better conditions. Israeli authorities did not fulfil their promises.

Multiple Prisons: 63 Days

About 90 administrative detainees launch a strike to protest their detention without trial or charges. Some 290 prisoners join, 70 of whom are hospitalised during the strike. The strike is regarded as the longest in the history of the hunger strike movement. The prisoners end their strike after a deal with the Israeli Prison Service, with no solid promises.

Multiple Prisons: 40 Days

Approximately 1,500 prisoners from across six jails participate in a hunger strike to coincide with Palestinian Prisoners Day. The strike is led by Fatah leader and respected figure Marwan Barghouti. Prisoners' demands include installation of a public telephone in all prisons to allow communication with relatives, resuming bi-monthly family visits, allowing second-degree relatives to visit, increasing the duration of visits and allowing prisoners to take photographs with their families. A deal is said to have been reached with the Israeli authorities but the details have not been made public yet.

Source: https://www.aljazeera.com/news/2017/05/28/a-timeline-of-palestinian-mass-hunger-strikes-in-israel/

Picture References

Name	Source from Website
Cover	https://twitter.com/ImperialistWl/status/1221798439379439616/photo/1
Mohammed Alian	https://hadfnews.ps/
Frank Stagg	Bobby Sands Trust
Ismaat Mansour	https://palarchive.org/
Adeeb Mafarja	http://israeliprison.weebly.com/
Akram Al-Rikhawi	https://www.activestills.org/
Ayman Al-Sharawna	https://samidoun.net/
Gerry Kelly	Courtesy Gerry Kelly
Hanna Shalabi	https://shms.ps/
Dirar Al Hroub	https://asravoice.ps/
Hassan Safadi	https://www.shorouknews.com/
Khader Adnan	https://m.al-sharq.com/
Laurence McKeown	https://www.irishtimes.com/
Mohammed Al-Qeeq	https://www.middleeastmonitor.com/
Ali Asafra	https://felesteen.ps/
Rawda Habib	https://paltoday.ps/
Mary Doyle	Courtesy of An Phoblacht
Mansour Atif Rayan	http://www.elastal.ps/
Thaer Mahmoud Al-Kurd	https://alresalah.ws/
Mohamed Abdel Karim Abuataya	http://www.alaqsasport.ps/
Martin Ferris	Courtesy Martin Ferris
Zuhair Salah Al-Chechnya	http://www.hosh.ps/
Mohammed Hassan	https://www.alwatanvoice.com/
Mohammed Al-Dirawi	https://www.facebook.com/photo?fbid=1118887241457231&set=ecnf.100004373382967
Pat Sheehan	https://en.wikipedia.org/wiki/Pat_Sheehan_(Irish_republican)

Jehad Abughabin	https://www.facebook.com/%D8%AC%D9%87%D8%A7%D8%AF-%D8%A3%D8%A8%D9%88-%D8%BA%D8%A8%D9%86-%D8%A3%D8%A8%D9%88-%D8%AC%D9%85%D9%8A%D9%84--115906061927776/
Tarik Al-Modallal	https://www.palinfo.com/
Ali Almughrabi	https://felesteen.ps/
Tommy Mckearney	https://en.wikipedia.org/wiki/Tommy_McKearney
Walid Mahmoud Miqdad	https://www.facebook.com/photo.php?fbid=181400486673781&set=a.113267406820423&type=3

These books are available from the website below:

- *shop.ihrc.org/palestine*
- *kitaabun.com/shopping3/prisoners-diaries-palestinian-voices-from-israeli-gulag-p-5458.html*

- *shop.ihrc.org/dreaming-of-freedom-palestinian-child-prisoners-speak*
- *www.gerakbudaya.com/dreaming-of-freedom-palestinian-child-prisoners-speak*
- *ilhambooks.com/dreaming-of-freedom-palestinian-child-prisoners-speak/*

These books are available from the address below:
An Fhuiseog, 55 Falls Road, Belfast, BT12 4PD, Ireland.
Telephone: +44 28 90243371
Facebook: An Fhuiseog/The Lark

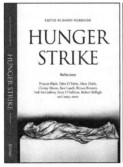
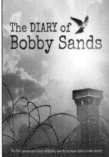
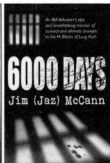